THE PATH FORWARD

A SHIFT INTO A NEW ERA

Don Durrett

The Path Forward

(Fifth Edition, February 2026)

Copyright © 2020 by Donald David Durrett
All rights reserved.

ISBN: 978-0-578-71317-5

WWW.**DONDURRETT**.COM

Books by Don Durrett

Post America: A New Constitution

The Demise of America: The Coming Breakup of The United States, and What Will Replace It

Kern County: The Path to Secession and a New Constitution

America's Political Cold War

How to Invest in Gold and Silver: A Complete Guide with a Focus on Mining Stocks

Get Healthy / Stay Healthy: A Practical Guide for Good Health

A Stranger From the Past

Conversations With an Immortal

Finding Your Soul

Finding Your Soul Workbook

New Thinking for the New Age

Spirit Club

Last of the Gnostics

The Gathering

Ascension Training

Team Creator

The Way

Your Soul Explained

Very few are expecting what is coming.

– Author's observation

Namaste: I bow to the divine in you.

– Hindu word

There comes a time when one must take a position that is neither safe, nor politic, nor popular – but one must take it simply because it is right.

– Martin Luther King Jr.

The Path Forward

Contents

Introduction vii

Chapter One
Consciousness Shift 5

Chapter Two
Economic Shift 27

Chapter Three
Political Shift 43

Chapter Four
Cultural Shift 57

Chapter Five
Healthcare Shift 65

Chapter Six
Spiritual Shift 75

Afterword 91

Book Review Request 93

Introduction

The title of this book is *The Path Forward*. That path is unknown because we are creating it together. The future is fluid and constantly changes based on our collective consciousness and collective decisions. But what I do know is that a better world is coming. The light (or a higher vibration) is expanding in our collective souls and is steadily displacing darkness on the planet. For this reason, our future is bright, both figuratively and literally.

How do I know a better world is coming? Because the truth is going to be released, or more accurately, the truth can no longer be hidden. Humanity is waking up from its spiritual immaturity and spiritual naivete.

Here are some truth bombs. These are not ideas or beliefs, these are truths.

Objective truth exists.

What is true is always true.

Separation is an illusion.

Separation is a lie.

There is no separation between anything.

Nothing exists in isolation.

Everything is connected by consciousness, and everything is conscious.

The reason separation does not exist is because there is only one consciousness.

We all share the same consciousness.

All is one.

That one consciousness is the Creator (or God).

Because there is only one consciousness, God is us, and we are God.

Nothing can exist apart from the Creator.

Earth is a school where souls evolve, and God gets to evolve through us.

Earth is on the physical plane, which is an illusion.

The Earth is similar to a computer game where we are the avatars (neither is real).

The only thing that is real on Earth is our souls, which are pure energy.

The physical plane is simply energy vibrating at high rates of speed.

Our bodies are vibrating at around 100,000 cycles per second.

The purpose of the physical plane is for the Creator to experience life in physical form.

We are all students. No one is not learning. That's why we are here.

We are God's surrogates. We are basically avatars, wearing a mask and playing a role.

The purpose/meaning of life is the expansion of life.

Very few people today are aware of the truth, but that is about to change.

Nearly everyone today is content to pretend that they are humans.

We are not humans. We are eternal souls in a human body.

Soon civilization will begin to recognize who we really are: eternal souls.

It is extremely rare for someone on this planet to be experiencing their first incarnation.

Introduction

The vast majority of people on this planet have incarnated hundreds or thousands of times.

Everyone has a soul, and it was not created for this lifetime (you have lived before).

Souls are aspects of the creator and are eternal.

The core of our soul is love and is the basis for all of our lessons.

* * * * *

I'm an old soul and have been writing about the transformation of humanity since 1990. Back then, my writing about the future was based more on hope and faith than knowingness of the outcome. I had a knowingness of my soul, but not necessarily knowingness of the future of humanity. Today, I can say that the future has changed for the better. Humanity is evolving spiritually in a good way, and that direction is going to continue to be positive. Today, there is nothing that can stop the truth from coming out. It is inevitable. The truth shall literally set us free and create a unity consciousness.

That unity consciousness will not happen overnight and will take a few generations to complete. But we will see its nascent beginnings and know that we were the generation that put it in motion. We will feel a certainty that what we put in motion will culminate. We will have no doubts about the outcome, which will be an incredible feeling of achievement. We are the progenitors.

Today, it may not look like humanity is evolving toward unity consciousness. In fact, it currently looks like the opposite is occurring. There are protests and refugees throughout the world, and wars are lingering in the Middle East, Asia, and Africa.

However, signs of peace are also there to see. War in Central and South America is at an all-time low. Plus, the Internet is steadily exposing evil and darkness in the world, such as the sexual abuses exposed by the #metoo movement, racial discrimination, human trafficking, pedophilia, and other human rights abuses.

This book explores how humanity is steadily moving toward the light and away from darkness, and how that will impact our future. It is a metaphysical book and includes a fair amount of "woo-woo." You may have to expand your awareness and belief system to accept some of these ideas, especially when I write about the consciousness shift in Chapter One.

* * * * *

I just made a statement that I should clarify. What does moving toward the light and away from darkness mean? We are light beings. Not only is our soul pure energy that glows as light, but the cells in our body also generate light. Science is starting to understand that we create light internally. This occurs because our cells are literally creating electronic charges and electronic signals. These charges create light, and the higher we vibrate, the more energy and light we create. Moreover, as we become more spiritually aware, our bodies become less dense as we vibrate higher and generate more light. This is what I mean by moving toward the light and away from the density of darkness.

The light is love, and the absence of love creates the darkness. The reason darkness (evil) is so prevalent on this planet is due to the lack of spiritual awareness. Some religions say that it is a battle between good and evil. That is somewhat accurate. However, what they get wrong is that evil is not bad from the

Introduction

Creator's perspective. The lack of light is simply souls who have not yet learned that their core is love. Evil (darkness) is simply the lack of love (light).

My favorite analogy of how God teaches us that love is a flame ready to be ignited is a depressed dog in a shelter. The dog is completely miserable. But if you take it home and love it, it will come to life. A human is the same.

Evil can be removed by adding love (light). Evil is simply live spelled backwards. Do you understand the connotation? God has a sense of humor. With enough light (love), you can remove all of the evil from the world.

The reason we judge people who are evil as bad is from the belief that they are separate from us and separate from God, the Creator. This is simply not true. Separation is lie, a misperception. Separation cannot exist because there is only one consciousness. This is not my belief. This is the truth. The truth is always true. I don't believe there is only one consciousness. I know it. I am a gnostic. I have the ability to know the truth, and so will most of you in this lifetime. Once you experience the truth, you can't unknow it.

* * * * *

I will be making projections into the future that are based on my expectations and from sources that many consider unreliable, such as channeled information. I will likely be proven wrong most of the time, but in many cases, I will be correct in the general outline of what is about to unfold.

My purpose for writing this book is to reveal the spiritual shift that is currently unfolding on this planet, and to give you confidence that the eventual outcome will be worth any hardships you have to endure during this decade, and future decades. It won't be a smooth path to peace and harmony, but it will be worth it.

The second purpose for writing this book is to give you the incentive to help. There will be a myriad of ways to help during this transition into a new era. Everyone will get to choose how or if they will help. Once the changes begin (and the truth is released), everyone will become aware that a transition is underway. If you read this book, it is unlikely that you will sit on the sidelines and not help in some way. After being exposed to what is coming, it will be difficult to ignore your responsibility to help. Even if you choose to stay on the sidelines, you will now consciously see it unfold from a wider perspective and understanding.

I would love to move to Maui and relax in retirement. However, my higher self has told me, nope, that is not your path. You came to help, and that you shall do. Darn the bad luck!

As the saying goes, you can't unknow the truth. Once you know it, you will want to share it. Many of you are probably rejecting many of the ideas you just read in this introduction, but once they become widely known, you will remember, and the light will go on. You will be forced to say, holy crap, he was right!

The third purpose of this book is to create a bridge of knowledge, whereby the spiritual is integrated with all aspects and areas of your lives. Some of you will not enjoy reading all of the topics. The reason for this discomfort is that I will be intertwining spiritual knowledge with modern economics, politics, and social systems. These are not topics that are normally combined. However, in order to understand where we are going as a civilization, they must all be discussed.

Chapter One

CONSCIOUSNESS SHIFT

The consciousness shift that is underway is difficult to explain, but I will try. Words tend to fail when you try to explain consciousness. Consciousness is something that is nebulous, without form, and impossible to measure. Consciousness is energy. In fact, it is pure energy. I'm not talking about the energy that we use to drive our cars or power our homes, but the energy of our soul and the mass consciousness. The soul and the mass consciousness can be considered pure energy because they do not dissipate. They always exist.

The soul is connected to the mass consciousness, which can be thought of as a grid or field of energy. Thus, the mass consciousness is an energy grid whereby everything is connected consciously. And when I say everything, I am including organic lifeforms (soil, trees, plants, animals, insects) and inanimate objects (rocks, wood, metal, air, and water). Everything is conscious.

Everyone and everything is connected energetically through consciousness entanglement. The current generation of scientists will prove this. This entanglement can be thought of as the mass consciousness. And because the mass consciousness exists, nothing can exist separately in isolation. Moreover, all matter is conscious and connected to everything else. Everything on the planet is conscious and energetically connected.

To repeat, all consciousness is energy and is interrelated and interconnected. Moreover, all objects are conscious. You probably think this is impossible because a piece of wood or a piece of glass can't feel pain. But what if I told you that someone could use their consciousness to make that piece of wood move, or even disappear? How can they do it? By consciousness entanglement.

That previous paragraph is not yet understood by most scientists. To them, consciousness entanglement is an unproven theory. However, to metaphysicians, such as myself, it is common knowledge. Study the history of yogis in India, and you will find that what they are able to do is only explained through consciousness entanglement. For a yogi to make an object appear or disappear is child's play, and very easy for them to do using their consciousness.

What you need to understand is that the dynamics of this mass consciousness field is determined by our consciousness. This energy can literally do anything. However, it is only a potential until a soul, or the mass consciousness, manifests an outcome. Consciousness energy is only capable of doing what consciousness is ready to do. As the saying goes, there are no accidents. Everything we perceive is manifested in some manner.

The only reason why the human body ages or requires nutrition is that our consciousness believes it is required. There are people on this planet who do not age and do not eat. How? They changed the dynamics of their energy field using their consciousness. In regard to aging, they manifested a different outcome than the average person.

For the past thousands of years, since the time of Lemuria and Atlantis, the energy field (mass consciousness) on this planet has been somewhat static. During our modern era of the last 10,000 years, it has been very difficult for people to change their energy field. Instead, their soul vibration was pretty much the same from their first breath to their last.

That has now changed. Actually, it began changing in the 19th century, but today it has reached a level where we can now

Chapter One: Consciousness Shift

individually change our DNA. This gives us the ability to vibrate our individual energy field at a higher vibration. And, as we each vibrate higher, we can now activate our DNA.

Many people's DNA today is changing from 2 strands to 12 strands because we are vibrating at a higher frequency. Over the next few generations, we will change from vibrating at 80,000 to 90,000 cycles per second to more than 120,000 cycles.

Our DNA is in every cell of our body. Everyone's DNA has its own unique vibration (frequency), as does every organ in our body. We each have our own unique energy field, which is a macrocosm of vibrating energy and vibrating energy fields (microcosoms) throughout our body. These combined energy fields encompass our aura, which can be thought of as our soul, which is pure energy.

There are several parts to our energy field. First, there is our physical body, which is a complex vibrating energy body, with each organ having its own vibration signature. Next comes our subtle body, which is the aura that surrounds the body. Included in the subtle body are our chakras, which are spinning energy vortexes that enliven the body. Entwined with both the subtle body and physical body is the soul, which originates outside the body and provides an information conduit to interact with other consciousness.

The mass consciousness creates the entanglement through which we are all connected. In the 1960s, the energy field of the mass consciousness began to vibrate at a faster rate. This allowed more advanced souls to begin to incarnate on the planet, pushing the vibration steadily higher. Then, in 2012, we reached a threshold. You could also call it a change point. We reached a vibrational level that was high enough to push us into a new era. That new era began in 2013, but was not really felt in a big way until 2019.

I don't think it was a coincidence that right when humanity reached a vibrational level that supported dynamic DNA activation, the COVID-19 virus struck. It was in 2019 when humanity began to go in a new direction. Beginning in 2019, all humans now have the ability to activate their DNA to a higher level that is dynamic and no longer fixed.

Today, the average person vibrates at about 80,000 cycles per second, with many old souls vibrating at around 120,000 cycles. Many advanced souls could not come here (incarnate) until the mass consciousness could handle their high vibration rate. That time has arrived. As these souls incarnate, they raise the vibration of the mass consciousness.

Civilization, humanity, life itself, is all about vibrating spiritual energy! Once the planet reaches an average of 120,000 cycles, peace will break out, and then war will become rare. Incredibly, we are not that far away from achieving this outcome, perhaps by the middle of the next decade. But long before this is achieved, many will be expecting this outcome. I am one, and now some of you are as well.

Civilization achieving an average of 100,000 cycles or 120,000 cycles per second is now inevitable. And this is a beautiful thing. As humanity raises its vibration, lots of good things will occur. Initially, it will be very subtle. You may notice yourself becoming more compassionate toward others or feeling a closer connection to family and friends. This eventually will lead people to understand/recognize that separation is a lie.

As humanity vibrates higher, more people will acquire psychic abilities. The prevalence of telepathy will initially be quite shocking. By the end of this decade, it will be accepted as a common ability. This will make it much harder for people to lie, and much harder to believe in separation. Telepathy is proof that we are connected.

Chapter One: Consciousness Shift

One of my favorite outcomes from this new higher vibration is that humanity will begin to recognize that integrity and truth are the traits that humanity needs to move forward as a civilization. We will stop allowing our leaders (both in government and business) to abuse their positions of power if they are not coming from a place of integrity and truth.

Also, individual freedom will soon be seen as a requirement for humanity. The soul has free will, so the individual must also have free will. Subjugating freedom will be seen as tyranny. This will lead to countries such as North Korea and China abandoning the repression of their citizens. We will get new forms of government and business that serve the people and not subjugate them.

It's a new world. Welcome to the new era. Those who become aware of this new vibration will know it. Some of those around them will notice a positive change, and some won't. Humanity, as a whole, won't notice for a few years. But, steadily, more and more people will become aware of this new consciousness. And, as they become aware, they will impact the mass consciousness for the better. Light (love) will steadily replace darkness (the lack of love). Love will steadily replace hate. A new world, a new era, is being born. The truth is being released: we are all one.

The energy field of the mass consciousness has now shifted higher to the point where it is now vibrating high enough that nearly anyone can change their energy field. People can now raise their vibration high enough to activate their DNA to 12 strands of dynamic DNA. This is truly a historic event in the cosmos, and the most significant event to occur on this planet in thousands of years, and perhaps ever.

What does it mean that you can now change your energy field and change your energetic vibration? The possibilities are nearly endless. Self-healing and slowing the aging process will become common in the near future. Many people will become more psychic and highly intuitive. Also, our behavior will change in a positive manner as we begin to recognize our connectedness to each other. This will lead to virtuous traits of being more compassionate, loving, grateful, humble, considerate, gentle, gracious, kind, and friendly toward others.

How does one raise their vibration and change their energy field? You do it with your consciousness, which has to become more spiritually aware. Ideas and beliefs have to be replaced with truth. The most important truth being that separation is a lie. You also have to connect with your higher self, which is your soul on the other side of the veil. You can do this by speaking directly (using telepathy) to your higher self and then listening (using telepathy) for direction. The key is knowing that your higher self is on the other side of the veil listening to you at all times (trust me, it is!). Then you wait for a response. This is how you learn to be spirit-led and highly intuitive.

After you accomplish learning how to be spirit-led (instead of being ego-led), your higher self will lead you to a higher state of spiritual awareness. This will lead to your cells vibrating higher and your DNA activated at a higher level. Currently, your DNA is likely operating at only around thirty percent. In this lifetime, you can increase it significantly, perhaps to thirty-five percent. Amazingly, this wasn't even possible for nearly all of humanity until 2019. Once a human reaches approximately thirty-three percent DNA activation, amazing things will begin to happen.

I know what you are thinking. Don, how do you know all of this stuff? I'm a fifth-level old soul, which is way up the continuum of awareness (it only goes to seventh-level old soul on the physical plane). Plus, I have the role of Priest and a sub-role of Scholar (not in human terms, but spiritual terms). I have lived many lives with these roles.

Chapter One: Consciousness Shift

As a Priest-Scholar, I am an ideal soul to grasp this spiritual knowledge and to be led to it. One astrologer read my natal chart and told me she was amazed at my potential for spiritual understanding. She said it was unlimited. Trust me, I'm not making this stuff up.

* * * * *

Our soul is only partially embedded into our body. In actuality, our soul surrounds our body as an energy field. Again, this field is called our aura. Our soul is composed of indestructible, pure energy. The main portion of our soul exists on another plane of existence, which is non-physical. These non-physical worlds are also called spiritual planes or spiritual dimensions, sometimes called etheric planes. We currently live on the physical plane, which is an illusion and consists of vibrating energy that was only created for physical experience. The physical plane is analogous to a video computer game. It is the same concept: a temporary virtual reality, and we are the avatars.

By the year 2050, this will be proven by science. Scientists will be able to show how and why objects vibrate, how they are connected and interrelated, and that the density of an object can easily be manipulated.

Anything in the physical universe is an illusion. The only thing that is real is consciousness, which is non-physical. Consciousness can create and manipulate physical objects, but physical objects cannot create consciousness. Physical objects are created from consciousness. The soul is one form of consciousness, but so is a physical object. However, they are not the same thing. The difference is that a soul can evolve spiritually, and a physical object cannot.

If you think that I am making all of this stuff up, consider this: the Pleiadians (who will soon make themselves known), live with their DNA activated at eighty percent. On their planets (near the Pleiades constellation), they do not make objects from raw materials, such as steel and aluminum. Instead, they create whatever they need from consciousness. That is our future too, but it will take us generations to evolve to that level. However, within a generation, we will know, as a civilization, what I am writing about in this chapter.

*****

A physical object is alive and has consciousness because everything has consciousness. How can this be? Because everything is connected to the Creator. And since we are also connected to the Creator, we too, are connected to everything. Intuitively, we think this is impossible. We think it is a lie, when in actuality, separation is the lie. Separation doesn't exist. How can we be connected to the ground we walk on, the air we breathe, or the chair we sit in? How? Because it's interrelated energy.

We think that our bodies are solid and that the ground we walk on is solid. It is not. The truth is that it is possible for a human body to increase in vibration and walk through a wall. It's also possible for a human body to increase in vibration and move to another location instantly. That location can be somewhere else on this physical plane or even a non-physical plane. Consciousness makes this possible because consciousness can control the dynamics of energy, which is the foundation of life.

Chapter One: Consciousness Shift

When our soul leaves our body after this lifetime, we will once again exist in a non-physical world. These non-physical worlds are much vaster than the physical universes, and they are all controlled by consciousness, well actually, one consciousness, the Creator.

At all times during this lifetime, our soul remains connected to our higher self, which is the larger part of our soul. When we incarnate, we only take a small portion of our soul with us, because the human body cannot hold all of it. Said another way, the soul has too much energy for the human body to contain. As a side note, recognize that who you think you are is much vaster than you realize.

The important point to understand is that our soul is vibrating energy and connected to everything via consciousness entanglement. Everything on this planet is interrelated energy that encompasses the global mass consciousness. This global mass consciousness impacts each of us, and it sets the tone for our collective decisions.

The global mass consciousness consists of an overall vibration. This vibration is real, and it comes from the vibration of the collective. Kryon (channeled by Lee Carroll) started releasing information in 1989 and called this global mass consciousness the energy grid. He has also referred to it as the field. Kryon said that this energy grid was changing as humanity vibrated higher. He said this would continue and thereby impact the global mass consciousness in a positive way.

For the last thirty-five years, Kryon has steadily educated humanity about this energy field and how it is impacting civilization. He has meticulously explained how the energy field (mass consciousness) impacts our DNA and drives humanity to higher levels of spiritual awareness. The energy field is the Creator, and the Creator is leading us to a positive outcome: a new humanity based on love.

Science has not yet been able to prove the existence of this global mass consciousness energy grid. Most of the people who know about it are in the metaphysical community, such as myself, and now you. Steadily, over time, more and more people will come to learn about it.

The vibration of the global mass consciousness is an energy field that impacts everyone's soul. Our soul is connected to this global mass consciousness, which makes us connected to everyone else.

The global mass consciousness is all-encompassing and pervasive. You can think of this global mass consciousness as the Creator. It is the foundational consciousness of humanity and impacts everything. Moreover, as individuals become spiritually aware, they are able to collectively raise the vibration of the mass consciousness, thereby creating a consciousness shift and forming a new humanity. This is happening and will continue to happen. This is the truth of how the future is being formed by this generation. We are the founders of the new humanity, the new era.

Kryon has said that all it took to create this consciousness shift was for less than one percent of the global population to become aware of the truth of their being (what I am explaining in this chapter). Thus, a very small group of people was capable of creating enormous change for the betterment of humanity. And that small group is increasing in size every day as more people become aware of their soul and higher self. This can also be called enlightenment, which essentially means the ability to understand the truth that we are light (consciousness) beings.

This is a planet of free choice, so the Creator allows us to make our own decisions (also known as free will). This freedom of choice means that each soul decides when to become enlightened. For this reason, the future is not deterministic. Instead, it is based on the decisions we make today as individuals and as a group. And every decision we make in this lifetime as individuals is in some

Chapter One: Consciousness Shift

way related to the decision to become enlightened. Reread that last sentence slowly and let that fact sink into your noodle.

* * * * *

What is known at this time, since the future is not deterministic, is that the probabilities are extraordinarily high that this civilization is on the path to enlightenment. This probability is based on occurrences that have happened on other planets. Almost always, when a planet crosses a threshold of spiritual awareness on a mass consciousness level, the end result is planetary enlightenment. We crossed that threshold in 2012.

Will you become enlightened in this lifetime? It's possible. Now that the energy field of the global mass consciousness has increased in vibration, anything is possible. What you will need to do is to metaphorically flip the switch to change from an egocentric viewpoint based on beliefs to a higher-self viewpoint based on truth. Once you flip that switch, anything is possible.

Not everyone is ready to flip that switch. Living through the ego is what most people prefer, and they are not ready yet to turn that off. However, once you recognize that the ego is a dead end, you will flip the switch and begin to live through the higher self. And once you change to a higher self focus, there is no going back, because your awareness will expand. The ego will be recognized as a limited experience and soul-inhibiting. Your awareness of this limitation will drive you back to the higher self, which you will know is the only spiritual way forward. Note that it's perfectly okay for souls not to move forward spiritually in this lifetime. That is their free will choice.

The Path Forward

* * * * *

Now that the vibration of the mass consciousness has increased to the point where our DNA is now dynamic, more and more people will begin to have an ah-ha moment of the ego's limitation and the soul's limitlessness. People will begin to see that the soul (the higher self) is the only path to choose to move forward. Sticking with the ego will be a dead end.

For many, giving up the ego will be next to impossible. In fact, it will take four generations before everyone has chosen to be higher-self focused on this planet. The ego encompasses all of the temptations that make life so much fun. Giving up that fun for a higher purpose is not easily chosen. Most souls are not ready to make that change. It's a big change to decide to live for others (be in service to humanity) instead of living for yourself (ego-oriented).

Why would anyone want to give up the ego when it is so much fun? Because the ego is severely limited, and it's a dead end when those around you are exhibiting profound abilities. Those new abilities included enhanced intuition, self-healing, communication with your higher self, activating your DNA, mining your Akash (past-life experiences), slowing the aging process, and expanding your spiritual awareness. All of these abilities are only found through the higher self.

You might be content with your current life and don't care about these new abilities. Well, that is fine, but at some point, you will begin to recognize that if you truly want to help humanity, then the ego has to be pushed aside.

Getting in alignment with the Creator's plan (aligning with the truth) can only be obtained by following our higher self. Why? Because our connection to the Creator via our higher self is the

Chapter One: Consciousness Shift

only way to get that awareness. The ego is a trap because it does not have the answers we seek. As I said before, it's a dead end.

And what is the Creator's plan? It's really pretty simple. Once you learn the truth, as I have explained in this chapter, you will be ready to learn to love both yourself and humanity. That's it. That's the plan. And the ego will never lead you down that path. That said, we must have compassion for anyone stuck in the ego. We must recognize that, at some point, or in some future lifetime, they will flip the switch from being egocentric to higher-self-centric. To paraphrase what I have read many times, we need to love those who are stuck in the ego more than those who are not stuck. Why? Because they need more love and more encouragement. We need to be compassionate for their struggle.

* * * * *

Each individual can only make choices that are within their capability and within their Akash (past experience). For example, an individual may think they have the free will to spend all of their time having fun. In actuality, if all they do is pursue having fun, it will usually end badly. Their soul will allow them that experience for a while, but it is a dead end. Their soul knows, from their Akash, what needs to be learned in this lifetime, and the odds are low that having fun all the time is on the agenda.

An individual may think they have the free will to have fun to their ego's content, but what they really have is the free *choice* to experience the limitation of their free will. Unless we are in alignment with our higher self, what usually occurs is that we get to find out what doesn't work in our lives, and it usually ends badly. This happens because what the ego wants and what the higher self wants are usually two different things. Ultimately, it could take several lifetimes until the soul leads an individual away from the ego and toward the higher self.

What is important to understand is that the Creator does not care which choices we choose – there is no judgment. The Creator knows in advance all of the potential choices we can make, as do we at a soul level. We accept those potentials when we incarnate and do not perceive them as bad outcomes. Instead, they are lessons and, once they are learned, we can move forward.

Ultimately, the soul will evolve to a higher state of consciousness. This is inevitable because our core is love and connectedness. We can try to ignore this core using an egocentric viewpoint, but, eventually, it gets our attention. Why? Because each incarnation is planned with the sole purpose of evolving our soul. We don't incarnate to have fun; we incarnate to evolve.

When I say that our free will is limited, I'm talking about the soul's agenda in this lifetime. If the soul has an agenda that is counter to the ego's agenda, quite often, the soul (higher self) will prevent the ego from carrying out its plan. I am sure all of you have learned through experience that what you want and what you get are not always the same thing. That is the soul's agenda in action.

What the soul allows is for you to select from a limited number of choices to achieve an outcome. This is how everyone lives. We all have free choice to select experiences that fit within our agenda and align with our Akash. However, the soul is very diligent in limiting these choices.

Some people have a vast array of choices, while others have much fewer selections. Education and money can expand these choices, but conscious awareness can play an even larger role as a determinant. The more lucid one becomes in one's knowledge,

Chapter One: Consciousness Shift

the more opportunities arise. Conversely, if an individual makes poor choices, they can find themselves with very limited options.

The choices that individuals make can impact humanity in a profound way. The Creator allows humanity, as a whole, to decide the direction it wants to go through its free choices. Each of us, through our choices, gets to choose how humanity evolves. This is why humanity matters, and why humanity truly is one large family.

You can think of humanity as a democracy where everyone gets to vote through their life choices and beliefs. And since free will is limited, the Creator only allows certain outcomes. This is why civilizations in the past have been destroyed, and we had to start over. Lemuria and Atlantis are not fiction. They actually existed and were destroyed.

Atlantis made several bad choices that led them down a path of destruction. The current civilization also came close to a path of destruction during the 20th century. Luckily for us, we avoided another path of destruction.

This ancient history of the planet is fascinating, although few know about it. There is very little mainstream literature about the civilizations of the Lemurians and the Atlanteans (to learn more, watch Initiation on Gaia TV with Matias De Stephano). And few know that the Creator has been planning for thousands of years the enlightenment of the current civilization, which we get to experience, or at least the beginning of it.

What is happening today is the result of at least 100,000 years of planning, and likely much longer than that. The consciousness shift that we are now experiencing has been ongoing for thousands of years. It began to speed up during the second half of the 19th century. At that time, esoteric knowledge was released on the planet in a big way. This is largely unknown, but if you do some research, you can learn about it. Perhaps you have heard about

Abraham Lincoln's wife attending séances? Those occurred during this timeframe when the shift in energy became more pronounced.

The consciousness shift that began in the 19th century continued into the early 20th century. At that time, there were yogis from India visiting America and spreading esoteric teachings. Krishnamurti was born in the early 20th century and came to America to live. His books and teachings impact people to this day. He was only one of many who introduced Eastern mysticism into the West. This was part of the shift that began to move the needle toward one percent of the population becoming enlightened.

As people become exposed to esoteric teachings, they become more spiritually aware. Steadily, as we progressed into the 20th century, spiritual awareness increased. This led to the 1960s, which was really the first major burst of global spiritual awareness. The 1960s created massive changes to humanity on a spiritual level.

After the 1960s, it took about two decades to steadily increase the planet's mass consciousness vibratory level enough to change humanity's destiny. Then, in 1987, we passed a significant vibrational threshold as a mass consciousness. This was celebrated as the harmonic convergence. At that time, humanity reached a vibratory level that effectively announced to the universe that this planet was going to evolve into a new humanity.

Incredibly, this harmonic convergence event and the spiritual achievements that have been made on this planet have largely been kept a secret from mainstream society. Those in the metaphysical movement are well aware of what I have written in this chapter, but for the rest of society, this is all new to them.

If you have followed my train of thought throughout this chapter, then you will grasp that what happened in 1987 resulted in what was perhaps the most pivotal year in human history. In 1987, the collective global mass consciousness changed the direction of humanity toward a more spiritually evolved planet. In 1987, we put ourselves on a path toward enlightenment, which the collective global mass consciousness agreed to pursue. Then, in 2012, we reached another threshold, and something amazing occurred: the human DNA changed for the entire planet. Not only did our DNA change, but it signaled more DNA changes to come. Today, our DNA has literally become dynamic. It's as if someone had flipped a switch.

In many respects, the changing of the DNA in 2012 was the most significant event to occur on this planet in thousands of years. That change is going to allow us to evolve spiritually to a level that is beyond our comprehension. That change is now underway.

DNA is energy and consciousness. So, when the DNA changed, there was also a consciousness shift, which continues to impact humanity. Our DNA now has the potential to be further activated, but it is up to each of us individually to activate those potentials. The old souls will be the first to activate these new potentials. They will begin displaying those abilities that I listed previously.

Many will now begin to activate their DNA to operate at a higher level than thirty percent. This will cause a huge shift in civilization over the next few generations – all for the better.

* * * * *

As mentioned before, when the soul comes into the human body at birth, the majority is left behind because the human body cannot contain the entire soul, but only a small portion. The remainder of the soul exists on another plane of existence and is not constrained by the ego or physical reality. The part of the soul that is outside of the body is usually called the higher self.

There are several levels of intelligence that are available to us: our human brain, our higher self (the soul), and our innate body. In fact, you could consider even more levels of intelligence, because the soul allows us to communicate with spirit guides (sometimes called guardian angels) and discarnate beings for guidance. Also, our higher self (the soul) provides us with intuition, which is also a form of intelligence.

Another fascinating aspect of the soul is our Akash. The Akash is the history and experience of our past lives, which include *all* of our past experiences. As we become more closely connected to our higher self, we have access to our Akash. Anything that we have learned in prior lifetimes can be accessed in this lifetime.

I'll give you an example. If you lived a healthy past life, you might find yourself changing your diet and suddenly becoming healthy in this lifetime. This is from remembering a past-life experience and putting it into action. This will be very subtle, and you won't actually remember the past life. Instead, your intuition will guide you toward a new diet and lifestyle.

Another example is becoming an entrepreneur and starting a business. If you have done this successfully in a past life, it will be much easier in this lifetime. This is why so many people are successful in starting and running a business. They intuitively *know* they can do it and have done it before. Other examples are musicians and artists. They come in naturally gifted from past-life experiences.

I need to explain the higher self in more detail because that is the means for accessing our Akash. Our higher self is the gateway to a vast array of knowledge and communication. The higher self connects us to the rest of our soul, to the Creator, to our spirit guides, to our Akash, to the collective consciousness, to our intuition, and to so much more. As more and more people tap into their higher self, humanity will evolve spiritually. In a nutshell, that is what

Chapter One: Consciousness Shift

is happening today on this planet on a massive scale, and it has been happening on a widespread basis since 1987.

The higher self is the gateway that activates our DNA and expands our DNA utilization. The average person on this planet uses about thirty percent of their DNA. Our DNA is now dynamic, and our utilization level can increase. It is no longer static, as science believes, and as we open our higher-self gateway, we can activate more of our DNA. This is happening today!

The future for humanity is that we will steadily increase the utilization of our DNA. In fact, we are on the precipice of becoming more quantum as individuals. Our DNA is quantum, but until 2012, most of us couldn't activate the quantum aspects of it, and it remained dormant. Some people today have already activated some of these quantum aspects, and it is a trend that will continue.

The potential of quantum DNA is limitless. However, it will take generations before we can activate our DNA to thirty-five percent as a civilization. But some of us will reach these levels in this lifetime. This is what will create a change for humanity.

If you increase the utilization of your DNA, then your life will improve in dramatic ways. Again, this can only happen if you drop your egocentric way of life and shift into a higher-self way of life. Why? Because only higher consciousness can change your DNA, and the ego does not want you to know how to do that.

Old souls will begin living longer because they will be able to communicate directly with their innate body. That sounds strange, but that is what our DNA now allows. Before 2012, we had very little access to the intelligence of the innate body. Now, that access is increasing. In fact, since 2019, it has become much easier.

With dynamic DNA, humans will now be able to heal themselves of diseases that, in the past, were considered untreatable. Again, not everyone will be able to do this at first. It will be the old souls who will lead the way and then teach others how to do it.

Another DNA change is that old souls will begin affecting others by emitting more light (indeed, we are light beings!). This won't be consciously apparent, but it will still happen, and these subtle changes will impact others. This is how light (love) will spread.

As love and light spreads around the planet, the dark energy (evil) will have nowhere to hide. This is how light energy (love and integrity) replaces dark energy (selfishness and corruption). It's already starting with the exposure of morally corrupt individuals. This will increase throughout this decade, leading to a new trend of truth and integrity. That will be the new foundation of humanity. That is the Creator's plan.

* * * * *

Perhaps the biggest change occurring today is that more and more people are beginning to interact with their higher self. The average person today, especially men, mainly interact with their brain (their ego). In the future, people will rely less on their brain and more on their higher self for guidance. The higher self is more intelligent than the brain because it has access to all knowledge – both the past and the potential future.

As I have stated, this consciousness shift has occurred and is occurring, although currently on a small scale. The consciousness shift is practically unnoticeable over short periods of time. However, over time, it will become more pronounced.

One of the biggest changes that has occurred to the DNA is that children are now being born with more compassion and a strong connection to their higher self. This is God's way of creating peace on earth. Within a generation, this will become noticeable. The children born since 2012 are wiser and more compassionate than those born previously. You will not be able to get this new generation to kill others. Wars will effectively be over soon because young people will no longer fight wars to kill others.

Instead of fighting wars, this new generation is going to find ways to help humanity move forward. This is the generation that will discover the physics of consciousness and make huge advances in science and technology. We are now entering the Aquarian age and leaving the Piscean age. Aquarius is known as the sign of genius and is associated with science, inventions, and technology. The technological inventions will come fast and furious during the next few decades. However, the most important scientific breakthroughs will occur regarding consciousness.

Kryon said that humanity crossed the knowledge barrier in 2019 (there was literally a barrier on this planet that prevented us from learning about consciousness as a civilization). This means that today nothing can stop us now from understanding the physics of consciousness. Once consciousness is understood, it will change everything. We will no longer need devices, vehicles, or machines of any kind. Why? Because consciousness can replace all of them. Of course, this will require several generations before all of this comes to pass, but it is on the way.

Kryon will not say when we will fully understand consciousness, only that it is now inevitable. He also said that soon this planet would be off-limits to dark entities. He seemed to imply that evil will steadily be pushed off the planet from the presence of light.

This consciousness shift that is underway has huge implications for humanity, all of which are positive. So, even though evil and darkness are still thriving on this planet, their influence is steadily diminishing. The light on the planet is spreading and will continue to spread. I don't know how long it will take, but I expect to see an improvement in my lifetime, and perhaps this decade. Light is winning.

For those of you who are interested in tapping into your higher self, read my book, *Your Soul Explained*. It will give you an insight into how to make that happen.

Chapter Two

Economic Shift

The combination of the COVID-19 virus, which began to impact the world in early 2020, and the Ukraine War, which began in February 2022, signaled the end of U.S. global hegemony. It's currently February 2026, and this is not yet apparent to everyone, but it will be soon. No longer is the U.S. economy and U.S. dollar strong enough to dominate global trade. Today, about 55% of international trade is done in U.S. dollars, and the dollar dominates reserve currencies held by foreign nations (about 57%). That dominance is about to decline rapidly.

While COVID and the Ukraine War were the trigger, the pressure had been building since 1971, when President Nixon took us off the gold standard. Since that time, the U.S. adopted an economic strategy of globalism in tandem with debt expansion (money printing). It was only a matter of time before debt became unmanageable. Today, our national debt has reached $39 trillion (debt to GDP is 122%) and is growing at $2 trillion per year. More importantly, we have reached a point where cutting spending is no longer an option because it would crash the economy.

The ramifications of this economic shift for the U.S. will be massive. The U.S. economy will stall. Jobs will be lost. Bankruptcies will proliferate. Worst of all, the economy will not come back to life. There will be a plethora of empty office space in all the large cities. We will begin to experience a new normal. America will begin to flounder. Actually, it already has begun to flounder, for those with eyes to see.

The new normal will lead to a myriad of changes to the economy and to our lifestyles. Initially, this change will be for the worse as our standard of living begins to decline. Supply chains will break down. Reliable services will become less reliable. Crime will increase. A sense of safety will become fleeting. However, as the years go by, we will begin to create a new economic system that is more humane and works for everyone.

I expected the economic weakness we are experiencing. What I didn't expect was a virus to be the pin that popped the "everything" bubble. I knew that, at some point, something would pop it. In fact, I wrote an entire book, The Demise of America, that was largely focused on what was coming economically. On the cover of that book is a dollar bill that is ripped in half. The premise is that the collapse of the dollar is coming, and that outcome is inevitable.

I don't want to rehash the current economic system or why the economic shift is going to happen. You can read *The Demise of America* for that explanation. Suffice it to say that politicians don't understand economics but have the political power to do whatever they want with monetary and fiscal policy. Capitalism was undermined because it was the politically expedient thing to do. Once you have the ability to print money, moral hazard is just waiting to happen.

America has created a mountain of debt, ignoring the fact that debt inevitably leads to a financial crisis that can destroy a nation's economy. History is littered with example after example of countries that overstepped their ability to manage their debt. America, in its hubris, thought it was immune, which, of course, it is not.

This year, the Federal Government will spend nearly twice what it receives in tax receipts. Debt has now become such a big problem that it dominates the U.S. economy and economic system.

Chapter Two: Economic Shift

Debt is the problem, and it's not going away. The die has been cast, and nothing is going to stop it from blowing up the economy.

The economy has already begun to break down. This is apparent from the massive manipulation of the economy by the Federal Reserve (U.S. central bank). Free markets are now a thing of the past. Also, it's not just the U.S. central bank that is manipulating its economy, but all of the large global central banks. The global economy has become unstable because of mass quantities of debt, and central banks have stepped in to prevent their economies from imploding.

The debt explosion is a sign of structural change that is about to occur. Ray Dalio calls this a new global monetary order, which is a good description of what's coming. Anyone who follows the global economy realizes that we have a debt problem. We are seeing protests throughout the world, where people are demanding economic changes. The protests have been pervasive and seem to never end.

In the U.S., about half of the workers make less than $33,000 per year, and discontent is rising. People recognize that income inequality is a problem that is only getting worse. You may think this is not related to the consciousness shift, but it is. As people become more spiritually aware, they will demand equality and fairness. Many inherently already know that we are all connected and all one. Humanity is rising up and demanding to be heard. This trend will not stop until there is a significant structural change to the economy.

The riots during the COVID-19 pandemic following the George Floyd death (a black man) by a white police officer, was more than just about racism. The resulting proliferation of looting throughout the country was also an outcome of economic injustice. Yes, people were angry that another black man was killed at the hands of a white police officer, but that anger encompassed more than just racial justice.

The COVID-19 pandemic is likely going to spur on economic structural changes. New ways of organizing businesses will be introduced all over the world. Many corporate cultures will slowly switch from a shareholder focus to an employee focus. Shorter workweeks and higher average pay will steadily become the new norm throughout the world. There will be a shift to address income inequality and quality of life issues.

UBI (universal basic income) will become pervasive throughout the world. The first country to announce UBI during this COVID-19 outbreak was Spain. Many other countries gave their citizens money to get through the crisis. These types of income distributions will become more common.

We will start to see corporations and businesses use a narrower salary structure. Instead of executives (the C-Suite) getting the bulk of the salaries and exorbitant paychecks, there will be a narrower pay band so that people are paid more equally. Instead of ten pay levels, some companies will have five or less, and the levels will be in a tighter range. Moreover, pay structures will be more transparent instead of today's cloak of secrecy. The pay bands will be public knowledge so that there is more transparency in regard to equality.

For those people who desire exorbitant incomes, they will be free to pursue starting their own businesses. Self-employed people will have the opportunity to make more money on their own. A business owner will have the opportunity to make an above-average income, and perhaps significantly above average, if he owns more than one business. The average worker will do much better than they do today. They will work less and get paid more. There won't be as much of a pay gap between a supervisor and an entry-level employee because of tighter pay bands.

Chapter Two: Economic Shift

Some people will live in communities that do not use money. Citizens in these communities won't even get paid a salary. Instead, the community will collect the income and pay all of the bills. This will be an option for people who are satisfied with a simple lifestyle without many amenities.

Society will evolve into more diverse ways of living, with some communities focusing on a sustainable lifestyle that could be considered hyper-localization. These communities will try to provide for all of their needs without much need for trade. Other communities will be more dynamic, with a focus on technology, trade, and innovation.

Over time, humanity will come to realize that each corporation or business is responsible for the caretaking of the community. This realization will force companies to recognize that everyone in their community is one of their stakeholders. These stakeholders will be acknowledged in their business plans and through company behavior. This will create a big shift.

Today, most companies focus on making money for their shareholders and/or top management. Soon, companies will exist for employees first and other stakeholders second. One of those important stakeholders will be the community, and the community will come before the shareholders, who will move to the back of the line in importance. In fact, most companies will cease having shareholders and will raise money from banks instead of equity markets.

A clear objective for humanity will be a work-home balance, with a focus on quality of life. People will recognize that society should exist to help and serve people. And what do people want most? Their freedom and their ability to enjoy that freedom. We are not here to overwork ourselves and never enjoy our lives. Society should exist to help people enjoy their lives. This recognition will create a shift toward more worker empowerment, and less corporate empowerment.

Each individual's quality of life will take on importance. Society will begin to care more about quality of life than the pursuit of wealth. This shift will move us to focus more on sustainability instead of growth. A question we will ask is, what is more important, our quality of life, or a focus on economic growth? The former will win.

Workers will be allowed to have more time off and utilize flex-time to their advantage. Many workers will choose to work from home part of the week, utilizing the Internet and technology to connect workers together.

In many respects, the Internet has already become the heart of the economy. The Internet's ability to transmit information has become critical to the economy and will remain so. Retail purchases on the Internet have simplified our lives and saved us a tremendous amount of time. That will not only continue but increase in importance. All transactions of money will be done electronically through the Internet. Shipments will be scheduled and tracked through the Internet. Marketing and interacting with customers will also be done through the Internet.

The largest boon to the economy will be free energy (we will call it free energy, but the devices that generate free energy won't be free). Free energy is not that far away from becoming a reality. Already, inventors have figured out how to move energy in a loop using magnetics. Other inventors are working on plasma technology, such as the SAFIRE project, which is essentially free energy. It is only a matter of time before these inventions are available for commercial use.

Free energy opens up vast possibilities for economic development. Food production, shipping, and transportation will

Chapter Two: Economic Shift

all will become less expensive. Also, housing utility bills will drop dramatically. Free energy devices will also make it easy for small communities to form off-grid. This will be a major trend as big cities empty out from crime problems and economic stagnation.

I don't know when free energy will become mainstream, but it's coming soon. It will be part of the economic shift. In addition to free energy, there will be a multitude of new inventions, such as AI (artificial intelligence) robots and AI software. These will lead to new industries and new types of jobs. One such invention will allow salt to be separated from seawater at a very low cost using nano-technology. This invention will solve our freshwater problem.

You may be thinking that, if we have free energy, an abundance of fresh water, and an abundance of food, the population will explode in size. Ironically, that will not be the case. In fact, the global population will soon begin to contract. The reason for this is the consciousness shift. As the vibration of the mass consciousness increases, not everyone will be able to handle it. Unless your DNA can adjust to handle the higher vibration, your life will come to an end through some form of disease.

I do not know the speed at which the population will decline or the overall number of people who will leave the planet early, but it will be dramatic. I would expect the overall population to drop by at least half over the next century. This population decline will continue for the next hundreds of years, eventually dropping the total below one billion people.

Yes, the planet is going to begin to depopulate. But I don't think that is something we should dwell on. Let's focus more on the positive.

One of the wonderful things about the consciousness shift is that work is going to become more enjoyable for the average person. Future work environments will be much more harmonious.

People will feel respected at work and feel part of a team, with many enjoying a family-like relationship with their co-workers.

When these economic changes begin, it won't be apparent that they are closely related to the consciousness shift that I explained in Chapter One. The consciousness shift will be a subtle underlying driver that pushes humanity to adopt a new way of organizing work and business.

Unfortunately, this harmonious work environment won't happen overnight. It will take a few generations for this to unfold as society steadily shifts. We are the generation that gets to initiate these changes, but it will not be a smooth transition because change is never easy. It will take an abundance of leadership and foresight. The key to getting these economic changes underway is to begin implementing new business practices that respect and empower workers.

Eventually, society will accept a new business philosophy in which workers come first. One of the foundations for this new business philosophy is that companies will no longer be allowed to hire entry-level employees at a salary level that is a tiny percentage of the CEO's compensation.

In the future, the average worker will work fewer hours and make more money. Plus, they will have the flexibility to try different occupations. If someone wants to take a paid sabbatical for a quality-of-life choice, then that will be provided. These sabbaticals will not be allowed every year, but perhaps every three to five years. People will take a year off to learn a new profession or to travel for a new experience.

If workers are not happy, they will have the option to vote out upper management. While a company may have a board of directors, it will also have a board of employees. This secondary employee board will have the power to make changes to the company and hold employee votes for specific changes. However, these votes will require a high threshold to be successful, perhaps as high as ninety percent.

These new business structures will not be dictated by government, but by smart businessmen and businesswomen, who will recognize new ways to manage businesses that are more effective. Once there is a recognition that employees come first, new business structures will evolve to achieve that objective. A top-down structure will be perceived as archaic and unproductive to achieving society's goals.

While employees will be paid well and treated well, this does not mean they can do whatever they want. Employers will have the right to dismiss (fire) workers who are not productive. This will go to an arbitration board that will determine if the dismissal was reasonable and warranted. An employee will be given an attorney to argue their case, but if the employee is not seen as a harmonious fit within the organization, then they can be asked to leave.

Companies will have a primary objective of being highly functional. They will strive for improvement and efficiency. Settling for mediocrity and dysfunction will not be an objective. It will be up to the company to rectify poor performance. This should be possible with all members of the organization working together as a team. If the company needs outside help for professional advice, this will be sought out.

Companies will work together instead of competing against each other. If two companies produce a competing product, they will work with each other to determine who owns the current market share and how to divide future market share.

If companies produce similar products, it is encouraged that these companies work together to make both of the companies better. Sharing knowledge is encouraged for the betterment of all humanity.

There will be no patents, only shared information. All software will be open-source.

Companies will not focus primarily on revenue growth and profitability. The overriding business objective will be to take care of their current employees and to benefit the community. If that can be accomplished without increasing revenue and profits, then that is acceptable. It will not be the company's responsibility to add workers and grow the business.

If an employee feels that they are not being treated fairly, they can file an arbitration case against their employer. They can seek changes to their current role in the organization, or damages, or both. All arbitration cases will be made public. As this information is shared, businesses can get a better understanding of what employees desire.

Over time, stock markets and large corporations will become extinct. It will be recognized that they are not needed and tend to have an overall negative impact on humanity. Smaller companies will be seen as more dynamic and capable of performing anything a large company could accomplish.

Companies will be mostly self-regulating, except when state and national standards are required, such as in construction and accounting. There will be simple regulations for most companies that will be clearly stated and fit into a small pamphlet.

Business taxes will be very simple with a low corporate flat tax rate, with no exemptions or write-offs. The annual tax form will be a single page.

Companies will be expected to be a harmonious addition to the community. If a business neglects its responsibility to be a community stakeholder, then it will lose its business license. Being a community stakeholder will mean treating their employees with respect and not being a detriment to society. If an arbitration board rules that the business is a detriment, then they will lose their business license or perhaps be put on probation.

Many businesses will change the way bonus pay and profit sharing are allocated. Some will use a team approach, whereby all employees receive the same allocation and amount. For instance, if the CEO gets a $50,000 bonus, so does everyone else.

Some communities will make many of their service industries non-profits, such as cable TV, Internet providers, insurance, banking, finance, utilities, healthcare, and even housing.

Capitalism is great for generating wealth, but we don't want it to impinge on our quality of life. When you allow a profit motive to rule over industries such as cable TV, insurance, and healthcare, prices steadily rise, and businesses seek to make a bigger profit. Are those profits really needed? Perhaps not, if non-profits can fill the need.

Other countries have been successful in using non-profit healthcare. I think it is inevitable that we will try it as well. Capitalism is great for companies that make things, such as vehicles, electronics, home items, etc., but it is not great for everything. Just look at how much of a mess our financial system has become using capitalism. Banks are clearly not conducive to capitalism. They end up creating more harm than good, as they soak up all of the capital, which tends to concentrate instead of proliferate.

We have been so caught up in pursuing wealth that we have missed some of the problems with capitalism, for instance, real estate. It is easy to get wealthy in real estate because it is a necessity. It's good that people have gotten wealthy, but it has come at a cost. That cost is the high cost of housing that many can't afford.

These high costs in housing can be trimmed back by using a non-profit approach. For instance, all multi-family apartment complexes can be made non-profit. Rental rates can be determined based on the original loan and updated annually based on property taxes and utility rates. Profit can be stripped out, thereby making inflation negligible.

For single-family housing, rentals can be eliminated. Any single-family house that is not inhabited for twelve months can be auctioned off. This will keep housing costs down.

For mobile home parks, we can end the practice of land leases (rent). Prefabricated homes are supposed to be low-cost and affordable, but the land they are placed on often undermines that goal, using land leases (rent). Mobile home parks should have zero property tax or land rent, thereby providing low-cost home ownership.

Commercial real estate can also be non-profit. Starting a new business should be easy as long as you can raise the startup funds. The cost of renting commercial real estate should be low enough to support small businesses.

These changes to our capitalist economic system won't happen in the near term. They will evolve through experimentation by communities. After an industry is converted to a non-profit, society will see that it worked out well. So, another industry will be tried, and on and on. Only those industries that are perceived as problematic to society will be converted into non-profits.

Society will recognize (after the debt debacle) that government is the problem when it comes to economics. The last thing you want is government involvement with business, and the less government involvement, the better. Also, regulations need to be kept to a minimum for businesses to thrive. This will be the new norm.

Chapter Two: Economic Shift

The only thing government is needed for is to set the rules, and those rules should be simple to understand and limited in quantity. This will keep the government small, which ensures people's liberty.

Society will figure out that the two biggest problems for the economy are unbridled capitalism (for certain industries) and government involvement in business. The former can be solved using non-profits for certain industries, and the latter can be solved by keeping government small and regulations simple.

Instead of using the government to regulate business, each industry needs to be self-regulating, with employees overseeing their requirements as a community stakeholder. And when I say employees, I mean all employees. All employees are all responsible for self-regulating requirements. Their duty is to speak up if they see a problem. First, within the organization, and if that doesn't remedy the issue, to report it to the community.

We don't need a large, centralized government telling everyone what to do when we can self-regulate businesses. We can all be responsible citizens, and the benefits will accrue to all of society as a free nation.

Today, corporations and businesses have become too powerful. Employees are at risk of termination if they speak up, and their voice carries little weight. That needs to change.

We also don't need a banking system based on the expansion of the money supply, which inevitably leads to inflation. When you give a bank your money for safekeeping, it should not be considered an unsecured loan, which is how the current banking system works. Our money should be unencumbered if that is our choice. Fortunately, cryptocurrency will make this possible.

The banking system will bifurcate into public and private financial systems as cryptocurrencies are adopted. Initially, there will be the existing banking system, which relies on government-issued currency. In tandem with our current banking system, a new quasi-private banking system will arise, which will rely on privately-issued cryptocurrencies. This new system will be government-regulated, but the cryptocurrencies will be non-government-issued.

The crypto banking system will rely on digital wallets and smart contracts. Financial transactions will occur directly between two parties, without an intermediary. Banks will not be needed for these transactions. Instead, digital tokens (private money) will transfer directly between two parties. This is similar to when email replaced the need to use the mailman to send a letter.

Cryptocurrencies will proliferate for only one reason: they are needed. Our banking/money system has failed us, and crypto is needed to step into the void. In the near future, crypto will be an ideal solution that allows two private parties to exchange crypto as a means of exchange. It is the ultimate barter system, which is essentially the reason why money was originally created.

Old-fashioned banks will continue to exist, but they will no longer be based on fractional reserves, which was never a good idea. Instead, those giving money to banks will get a return on their money as an investment (similar to giving your money to a hedge fund or investment advisor). Banks will stop offering checking accounts, which will become archaic once digital wallets become the norm. Paper money will go away, as will paper checks.

To summarize the economic shift, society is going to create an economic system that works better for employees and, thus, society as a whole. That will be the objective, and it will be accomplished by changing our economic philosophy. Instead of businesses focusing on optimizing profit, they will focus on the stakeholders of the business, which will reverse the current hierarchy of shareholders first and employees last.

Chapter Two: Economic Shift

The shrinking of the middle class and the wealth concentration of the top 1%, has highlighted the economic injustice that is prevalent today. As society restructures to rectify and eliminate this problem, more opportunities and equality will be built into the new business structures. It will start with higher entry pay and better educational opportunities. Once society recognizes that all lives matter, a shift toward harmony will have begun.

What's beautiful about this future economy is that we are the generation that puts it in motion, and that is a wonderful thing to be a part of.

The future economic system will not be based on socialism, where everyone is perceived as having equal abilities. That's insanity, because no two people have equal abilities. We each have our own strengths and weaknesses. Recognizing these differences and assigning the best person for a task is what makes society thrive.

It is society's responsibility to allow people to develop their skills and abilities, and not to allow people to be neglected. The future economy will allow people to chase their dreams, and those dreams can be big or small. That is what freedom is all about, and freedom is what makes people happy.

If there is one word to describe the future economy, it would be freedom. People will be given the freedom to do what they want. They can choose to do nothing, or they can choose to work with others doing something they enjoy. Or, they can chase a dream and aspire to achieve something meaningful that satisfies their heart's desire.

Humanity will attempt to create the ultimate economic system: one that not only provides opportunity for all, but also is moral, holds integrity, and where people enjoy working.

The Path Forward

Chapter Three

POLITICAL SHIFT

We are currently experiencing the decay of our political institutions. Today, both parties (and there are really only two) are on opposite sides of many important issues, such as income inequality, immigration, healthcare, gun control, abortion rights, etc. It has gotten so bad that both parties no longer trust each other, nor want to discuss issues in a bipartisan manner. Clearly, our political system is broken and is not going to be fixed in its current form.

We have devolved to the point where the only way we can make a change of consequence is if a single party controls all three branches of the federal government. Consequently, gridlock has become the norm. Congress has been able to pass very few laws of consequence, other than budgets and bailouts, both of which were a necessity.

The Tenth Amendment of the Constitution was supposed to give state governments power. However, this amendment is largely toothless. America exists today as a centralized nation, where power resides in Washington, D.C. All economic policies of consequence are determined in Washington. And since America is an economically driven culture, nearly all power resides in Washington. The COVID-19 pandemic is a good example of this near total power, where red states (Republican-dominated) had to follow Biden's executive orders (EOs).

Perhaps the biggest shift coming in politics this decade will be the move away from centralized government based in Washington, and back to states and local communities (where states take back their power). Over time, all big decisions that impact local communities will be made locally.

Today, money is the ugly face of politics. Large corporations and billionaires have an overwhelming influence on what laws are passed. Lobbyist groups for the various industries, such as healthcare, banking, insurance, technology, manufacturing, food, oil and gas, telecommunications, aerospace, and many others, wield enormous political power because of their financial might. People may vote for elected representatives, but their voices are drowned out by the powerful lobbyists and their checkbooks.

So, the coming shift will take money out of politics, and politicians will begin to serve humanity and the people. This won't happen overnight but will steadily unfold over a generation or two. Corporations and those with an abundance of wealth will steadily become less influential and will be replaced by the voice of the people.

As lobbyists and billionaires lose their influence, politics will become more local as politicians become focused on local issues. Today, national politicians are more focused on national issues, leaving state and local issues to languish with low priorities. This is why education, mass transit, and homelessness problems have largely been ignored. State-level politicians do not have the means or political power to address these problems. For instance, can you name a single state that has attempted to address these issues?

I expect the coming consciousness shift to shatter our currently powerful national government. Over time, I expect the national government to wield less and less power. In fact, the country will likely break apart into a series of countries, as political differences create a chasm that cannot be crossed. These new countries will each create new political systems that are more aligned with local issues. Also, these new countries will adopt new political systems that are more adaptable to the needs of the people.

Chapter Three: Political Shift

What I have just described is the breakup of the nation. That will be the end result, and it will happen faster than you expect. Washington, D.C., will end up becoming a museum that is visited for nostalgia. Its influence and power will soon dissipate, and then shortly after, it will no longer be our central government.

The same dynamic that causes regions to secede and form new countries will drive communities to form new political systems that are locally driven. States will find that it is in their interest to allow these new local political systems to arise and evolve. Why? Because they will be positive for these local communities and for these new countries as a whole. Experimentation with politics will be all the rage once it begins. States are not going to create the same thing (centralized government) that they just abandoned.

As the country shifts away from national government, the influence of money and corporations will steadily subside. New influences will come from society's desire to focus more on community and on what people want, rather than on economic growth.

It should be noted that the main driver behind this will be the subtle influence of the spiritual/consciousness shift, as explained in Chapter One. People will be motivated to find a better way to live and will use our past failures, such as income inequality, housing unaffordability, corporate hegemony, and usurpation of individual rights, as guidelines to be avoided.

Historically, people were never asked what they wanted or were given the chance to have a voice. Instead, those with money and power made the rules. That's how it has always been, but that type of societal formation is coming to an end. Never before has society been asked how they think a company or corporation should behave. Well, that time has come.

The Path Forward

The political shift will not begin at the national level. Instead, states will begin to ignore federal rules, laws, and guidelines. This is how states will begin to take back their power. It will start slowly and then steadily gain momentum. This will be a stealth secession, with the actual secession requiring several years to culminate in a new country.

States will begin ignoring Washington because state-level problems will begin to mount, and Washington will not be providing answers. States will basically go their own way. There will also be a political chasm that creates a divide so large that States will feel a revulsion from the leadership in Washington. So, the split will occur out of need, but also from extreme discontent.

One driver of discontent has been the politicization of the legal system. No longer does the Constitution work as a basis of law. Our legal system has devolved into chaos that has become politically determined. Instead of creating Constitutional amendments to settle important issues, we have used politics instead. Hugely important issues, such as abortion rights, gun rights, immigration, and privacy, are now decided by the politics of the judges. There is no settled law to rely upon.

And to make matters worse, judges and politicians have begun ignoring the Constitution out of political expediency. In many respects, the Constitution has been and continues to be shredded. This has had the effect of ripping the soul out of the country. No longer does America have a common denominator that we all share. Our national values have become fragmented.

While the U.S. Constitution is a good basis for government structures and the division of power, there is nothing in the Constitution that defines appropriate corporate or business behavior. Instead, we have laws for what is not allowed, instead of what is expected. We have many laws for wrongdoing, but no framework for what society wants and expects. Without this

Chapter Three: Political Shift

framework, corporations do what they want without a hint of guilt, and rarely do CEOs go to jail. In fact, most of them get large severance packages when they are forced to resign for misdeeds.

The Constitution was written long before the Industrial Revolution. When it was written almost two hundred and fifty years ago, we had no idea how we wanted businesses to support society or their employees. As a result, today, we have corporate behavior that can be described as rapacious, avaricious, deceitful, corrupt, abominable, repugnant, yet perfectly legal. States will soon remedy this malfeasance through a direct compact between business and society. That is a shift that is coming.

No longer will corporations be allowed to lobby against changes that are in the community's interest. Today, if a community wants to implement government-based broadband for Internet access (to reduce consumer costs), corporations have been successful in stopping it (even if it is good for the community). The same corporate intransigence has occurred in regard to public transit, green energy, food labeling, etc. The list of intransigence against the public good is actually quite extensive, and politicians have allowed this to take place because of the money-based political system that currently dominates outcomes. A shift is coming that will stop this behavior.

One of the outcomes from COVID-19 was the experience of running out of necessities, such as food, toilet paper, paper towels, hand sanitizer, etc. This revealed what society had considered important prior to the virus outbreak. We had set up an economic system that was structured to generate maximum profits without considering the impact on society if supply channels broke down. Money (profit) was the driver, and humanity and the needs of the people clearly came second.

As a society, it is inevitable that we begin to shift toward the needs of the people and away from the profit-motive focus of the corporation. It has become steadily obvious that the power (and greed) of the corporation has become too extreme. The COVID-19 event was like a laser beam that focused society's attention on this misplaced power. People were being used by corporations, and it was clear for all to see. This is going to create a shift in politics that recalibrates the power structure back to the people.

Many people knew after the COVID-19 pandemic that we needed change with regard to corporate power versus our own well-being and personal rights. How did pharmaceutical companies get so powerful that they could get governments to force citizens to take experimental vaccines? However, corporations are not going to quietly relinquish their strong position in society without a fight. But the die has been cast, and changes to our political system are now underway. What pharmaceutical companies and the healthcare industry did in the name of profit will reverberate throughout all of corporate America.

Because of COVID-19, our political leaders (either at the national level or state level) must begin to rein in corporate power. This will require a change to our economic system, and once we begin modifying our economic system, it will be a slippery slope. Once we change our economic philosophy, there is no going back. And society knows what it wants, which is a larger focus on the needs of the people. The question of why a business or corporation exists will be asked for the first time in American history. The answer is obvious to everyone, which is to serve humanity. In other words, humanity comes first and not the corporation. People come first.

The economic question for the COVID-19 event is, how do we get people back to work? But this is also a political question. For the first time, we will begin to ask the question, how do businesses and corporations serve humanity and people? What is their responsibility for getting people back to work? In the current economic system, we do not burden businesses and corporations with this responsibility. Instead, we allow them to create their own plans and their own agenda, which they can do in their own pursuit of profits. In other words, businesses and corporations currently have more power than the people who work for them, much more.

This huge discrepancy in power will lead to a major political shift, as people desire change. And if they can't get it from the current political system, they will create a new one.

So, if our economic system is going to change, it has to impact politics in a major way. A trend/shift will be away from politics as power (money-based), and toward politics as service to humanity. Those who serve as politicians will strive to be of service to the community and the people. This is a huge shift away from the current norm. Steadily, career politicians will be supplanted by short-term politicians who want to be in service. It will be seen as a virtue to serve short terms. The reason why is because corruption is a moral hazard when you spend too long in office. There will likely be term limits in many places because of this hazard.

Once these changes begin, there will be a recognition that big government is not a good thing and needs to be limited. Small countries (regions) will prove that this is possible and will lay the groundwork for larger countries to emulate. As regions begin to secede and form small countries, they will make it a priority to limit the size of government. They will set an example for others to follow.

Self-governing by local communities and self-regulating by businesses will steadily become the norm. Societal problems will no longer be addressed using country-wide laws, but rather with local solutions. Instead of using the current model of writing a plethora of laws that are meant to nationalize certain behavior, society will begin to trust humans to behave, and then find local solutions when problems arise.

An overriding law will exist in some communities that will address something similar to disturbing the peace. If someone disrupts the harmony of the community, then they can be called to account for their misdeed. They will be treated fairly by their peers, but they could face harsh penalties depending on their actions.

This shift of focusing on community harmony will not be restrictive and will allow people to live as they see fit, guaranteeing their liberty and individual freedom. For instance, liberty will not be curtailed by governments dictating how people should live, which is the current agenda of WEF (World Economic Forum) and many other socialist agendas.

The ideal of freedom and liberty will be widely followed (in some regions) and respected as a revered societal value. However, if the harmony of the community is impacted in a significant way, then a line will have been crossed. The overriding factor will be whether the disruption is impacting the freedom and liberty of others. Also, this disruption must be an actual event and not a perceived threat.

Today, governments have become so paranoid that nearly everyone is under surveillance. Edward Snowden informed us of that reality, which has turned out to be true. This invasion of our privacy essentially ignores the 4th Amendment in the Bill of Rights. The 1st Amendment has also been eviscerated. A good example of this today is the lack of freedom of speech on large social media platforms, such as Twitter/X, YouTube, and Facebook. These have become de facto political organizations, determining who has a voice and who doesn't.

Also, even though the Constitution guarantees our right to assemble and march in protest, this right is consistently denied or repressed by authorities. No longer is this right guaranteed, and most protestors today are treated as violators of the public good. America has turned into a police state, and protesters are often beaten and arrested. Our freedom and liberty have clearly been limited, and people are not happy with this trend.

The political shift will be toward more liberty and less control. People will have the right to live in freedom as long as they don't disrupt others. Government and institutions, such as the police, businesses, and schools, will no longer get to define what is acceptable and unacceptable behavior at their whim. Instead, individual freedom will be respected.

The whole idea of freedom will be rethought, and this will occur on the political level. What is freedom, and what does it mean? Today, freedom means that you can do what institutions allow. Increasingly, this has reduced our freedom as government, businesses, and institutions have reduced what is allowed. Liberty has steadily been eroded.

This curtailing of our liberty is palpable today as government, businesses, and institutions have continuously usurped our freedom. We know this, and we don't like it. We want our liberty back, and this will be part of the shift.

Members of society want their sovereign rights. This was supposed to have been written into the Declaration of Independence by the words *Life, Liberty, and the Pursuit of Happiness*. But they were only words, and they lost their importance. As I mentioned in the previous paragraph, they were usurped. We traded our rights for our way of life, and then our way of life was compromised by COVID-19. This gave us a chance to rethink everything.

What have we given up? It turns out, quite a bit. The first to go was our privacy. Governments, businesses, and institutions know pretty much everything about us. Perhaps our medical records are private, but that's about it, and even those have probably been exposed. The next to go was our sovereignty, which was ripped to shreds after 9/11 when the Department of Homeland

Security (DHS) came into existence from the Patriot Act. The DHS was supposed to be focused on terrorists, but of course, that has been subjugated to focus on Americans who are perceived as a threat to the public good. It's basically a militarized police force standing ready in case anyone decides to protest or threaten the government's agenda.

With COVID-19, we found out that laws could be created instantaneously by governors and mayors, without the consent of our elected national representatives. It started when the mayor of San Francisco issued a lockdown order requiring everyone who was not considered an essential worker to stay at home. The mayor got to decide what was considered essential work.

The mayor's lockdown order was considered an immediately binding law, with enforceable fines for those who transgressed. Incredibly, a mayor had assumed absolute power to determine the rights of the citizens and businesses in their community.

The lockdown order from the mayor of San Francisco was effectively bankrupting businesses and people, but no one seemed to care. No one complained. No one protested. Everyone did what the mayor required. They followed the lockdown order. After that, governors and mayors had a field day throughout the country. They realized they could create any law that they wanted. The governor of Michigan went so far as to determine what could be sold at retail stores. In many communities throughout the nation, people were arrested and fined for not following lockdown orders.

That's just the tip of the iceberg of what we have given away to the government, as far as freedom and liberty are concerned. For instance, how many government agencies do you depend on? I can count several. And how many large corporations are you dependent upon? These large corporations are legitimized by the government and often usurp our rights. Large corporations might as well be called extensions of the government.

Chapter Three: Political Shift

This is the freedom we have today. We do what we are allowed to do. Compare how people lived before I was born in 1960. Before I was born, there were no large corporations, and the national government was still small. At that time, people could largely do what they wanted. When you compare eras, you get an idea of how much we have surrendered. Well, that is going to begin to reverse. Our liberty and sovereign rights are going to return.

To give society back its sovereign rights of freedom will require a change in political philosophy. More than that, it will require society itself to change. We will have to agree to give ourselves the freedom that we have given away. The starting point will be acknowledging where our freedoms have been lost.

A good place to start is the reduction of the military and the domestic militarized police. We will come to acknowledge that the military and militarized police are imbued with political power. We will also come to acknowledge that anything that is imbued with political power probably needs to be reduced or eliminated. Why? Because the only thing that restricts freedom is political power.

Next, we will begin to reduce the size of corporations in order to reduce their power and negative impact on society. Then, we will do the same with government institutions imbued with political power. They will be reduced in size, stature, and influence.

This shift toward removing political power won't happen overnight. It will require examples that can be replicated. But this is coming. You can count on it. Freedom and liberty will be the ultimate outcome of this shift.

We are on the precipice of many beautiful things happening. First, the consciousness shift will lead more and more people to connect with their higher selves. This will lead to a more compassionate society with much more integrity. Second, our workplaces will be more employee-focused, creating an increase in our quality of life. Third, our political system will be reformed to create more liberty and freedom.

These shifts will not happen all at once or to all of America at the same time. They will happen over time at different levels of change for each community, state, or country. There will be a vast diversity of change, with a lot of experimentation.

To give you an idea of some of the political experimentation, some communities will literally eliminate their elected politicians. Instead, they will require citizens to serve their community, much like we do today with jury trials. Citizens will be required to enter their work history, education, and skills into the community database. From this database, a list of nominees for various government positions will be selected to serve the community for a limited period at a time.

Another experiment will allow citizens to vote on laws. This voting will be done on the Internet using blockchain technology that creates a public ledger that cannot be modified. Society will find that blockchain technology is ideal for counting votes and creating an audit trial.

Citizens will get the opportunity to approve or disapprove of existing or proposed laws. They will also get the chance to remove or add items to their constitution. The thresholds to make these changes will be decided by the community, and it will likely require a high threshold to modify the constitution.

In some communities, states, or countries, citizens will get to decide what is taxed and even the tax rates. They will do this by voting on the Internet. Communities will get to decide how they are taxed. No longer will this be decided by powerful lobbyists. It will also be common to ban political advertisements. Without these advertisements, citizens will be forced to talk among themselves to understand proposed laws.

Chapter Three: Political Shift

One of the positive outcomes from all of this diversity of change is that citizens can move to communities that are in alignment with their beliefs. Everyone will be able to find a community that fits their lifestyle. Some will have a conservative tone; others will have a liberal, spiritual, or libertarian tone. There will be many political flavors. Each community will evolve to have its own personality and social structure.

* * * * *

I thought this chapter was over, and then I came across some writing that was attributed to Saul Alinsky. He is famous for publishing his book, *Rules for Radicals*, in 1971. The writing I found was titled the eight steps to create a socialist state. It is a hoax and was never written by Alinsky. However, his book, *Rules for Radicals*, is widely admired by Democrats and has led to many of these outcomes.

The author of these eight steps is unknown, but when you read them, you can see the direction America is currently going in and why a shift is needed. We need to go in a new direction that leads away from these outcomes.

1) Healthcare: Control healthcare, and you control the people.

2) Poverty: Increase the poverty level as high as possible. Poor people are easier to control and will not fight back if you are providing everything for them to live.

3) Debt: Increase the debt to an unsustainable level. That way, you are able to increase taxes, and this will produce more poverty.

4) Gun Control: Remove the ability of people to defend themselves from the government. That way, you are able to create a police state.

5) Welfare: Take control of every aspect of their lives (food, housing, and income).

6) Education: Take control of what people read and listen to, and take control of what children learn in school.

7) Religion: Remove the belief in God from the government and schools.

8) Class Warfare: Divide the people into the wealthy and the poor. This will cause discontent, and it will be easier to tax the wealthy with the support of the poor.

It is undoubtedly true that all of these have come to pass to a certain extent, and that the U.S. is on the verge of becoming a socialist state. It's time to turn that around and bring back our liberty.

While Democrats have blindly or naively supported laws that have ingrained these eight steps, Republicans also have dirty hands. Republicans have railed against these outcomes but have not provided any leadership or ideas to solve our pressing problems. Instead, Republicans have pretended that nothing is broken, other than that there are too many Democrats. Their rose-colored glasses belief that America is the greatest nation in the world (while it is currently floundering), and their intransigence in discussing possible solutions to our problems, is their Achilles heel.

Both parties are on their way out, or at the very least, are in for a radical transformation. The Democrats need to wake up to the fact that they are creating a socialist state that is removing our liberty and individual freedom. The Republicans need to wake up to the fact that they are not solving any problems with their conservative leanings.

Chapter Four

CULTURAL SHIFT

The cultural shift will not be the first shift to occur because the U.S. is so focused on making money. The first major changes will be economic and political, and then the cultural shifts will come after.

The biggest cultural change will be a move away from individualism and a move toward collectivism. This term currently has negative connotations for most people. However, this new form of collectivism won't be political but cultural. People will begin to feel a bond between each other, which will manifest in a variety of ways.

The first form of collectivism will begin in small communities that form to start something new. The newness will revolve around supporting the needs of people, which has been lacking for decades.

A big part of this collectivism will be in various forms of sharing. This has already begun on a certain level, with vehicle sharing (Uber) and house sharing (Airbnb), although this sharing model is currently more about making money than collective benefit. In the future, the sharing model will be based more on helping others and making society more harmonious.

This new collectivism will inspire more responsibility and not less. Those who are part of a community will feel inspired to act responsibly and help their community. Volunteer work will be pervasive, as more and more people reach out to support their community. This will only occur if people feel part of something, which will only manifest if communities become more compassionate than they are today. This may seem like hyperbole, but the consciousness shift will make this happen.

This will occur slowly at first in the new communities, but then it will gain momentum as more and more people feel connected to each other.

The fear that freeloaders will take advantage of a collectivist, sharing society will prove unfounded. Quite the opposite will happen, as people find their place in society. People will also find that collectivism creates a society with a better support system. Today, people fall through the cracks and end up homeless. In the future, people will find a support system that gives them a place to turn. The fear of being left with nowhere to turn will be removed.

Sharing will lead people to gather together. For example, today, we don't share food very often, except for perhaps potlucks at work or with our family. In the future, communities will eat together and share food. There will be plenty for everyone. It will be a big party. It will be a way for the community to come together as a whole. These community get-togethers will allow the community to discuss local issues and share political ideas.

Another cultural shift will be the move away from large urban cities and into smaller cities and communities. Small communities will prove to be much more adaptable and productive than larger cities. They will initially be safer, and the support network stronger. Many of these small communities will be much more productive than they are today because of the proliferation of technology that will be abundant. They will have everything they need to be productive.

One trend will be toward hyper-localization. This means that nearly everything will be done locally, especially food production and energy generation. There will be trade between communities, cities, and countries, but hyper-localization will be common. There will be a trend toward building communities that are self-sustaining. Each community will make an effort to generate their

Chapter Four: Cultural Shift

own energy and grow their own food. New technology will make this possible.

Another major trend will be toward community interaction and integration. This will be the opposite of what we have today, where neighbors do not know each other. Communities will work together, eat together, and socialize together. For many communities, it will be one large, extended family.

This interaction and integration will occur because our DNA is beginning to make us feel an affinity toward one another. We are literally going to fall in love with each other and will want to be around each other as much as possible.

A big trend will be to support local businesses and make sure they thrive. These will be considered community businesses that support the community. These local businesses will be protected with low taxation and other advantages that non-local businesses do not receive. If a local business can support the local community, then a non-local competitor will not be given a business license. Corporate chains will be forced out because their main benefit is to provide jobs, but conversely, they pull their profits out of the community.

If a non-local business disrupts local business, then steps will be taken to keep that business local. Local businesses will have the support of the community because they create the economic strength of the community. No longer will big corporations be allowed to come into town and take over the market, to the detriment of local businesses. The culture will shift to support local businesses first.

The shift to keep the community strong will reverberate throughout the economic, political, and cultural landscape. Society will be proactive at preventing the consolidation of power, be it economic or political.

Food production will change dramatically. Today, we rely on large corporate farms and international imports for our food. Soon, communities will give local producers an advantage because they will be more reliable. Indoor food production can be achieved year-round, where the weather has little impact. Plus, local food production will tend to keep the community healthier because of its freshness and high purity standards.

By changing to indoor farming, it becomes less labor-intensive and more conducive to robotic labor. This creates a much more reliable and stable form of food production. Many of these indoor farms will be co-op owned. In fact, many families will belong to these co-ops, where they grow their own food.

Another cultural shift will be the adoption of higher health standards. This will begin with clean water. Every community will be proud of its clean water that comes out of the tap. It will be tested regularly, with the results posted on a public website. The desire for clean water will come from public initiatives to keep the community healthy. Good health will become a priority in many communities.

Achieving good health requires a dual outcome. First, the community needs to support initiatives that support good health. Second, community members have to recognize their personal responsibility to remain healthy through good habits. This will lead to a significant cultural shift regarding health.

Clean air will also be a high priority, as it will reflect the community's high health standards. It will be uncommon to see dark smoke in the air. Most communities will not allow it. Carbon-based energy is in its last years and will be replaced by free energy that has a zero-pollution footprint.

Health will see a huge transformation and shift in our culture. Today, most Americans have some form of illness and are on some

Chapter Four: Cultural Shift

form of medication. Changing this state of affairs will require a cultural shift in how we approach health. This will require a separate chapter to explain in more detail.

Religion will also see a huge transformation. All religions will come to an end this century. This means all religions in their current form are about to come to an end. How can that be? Well, the truth will be released (as explained in Chapter One), which essentially makes religion obsolete.

What is that truth? Simply that we are all one (sharing the same consciousness), and that reincarnation is real. Moreover, we are each here to evolve our souls, and how we do it is our own personal responsibility and not the responsibility of anyone else. Thus, religion will become a personal spiritual path.

Religion will not immediately die, but it will begin to change. There will be a realization that the truth can only come from within, and that we each hold our own truth. As you can imagine, if this occurs, that means our beliefs will have changed dramatically.

As our beliefs change, our culture will change. And since Christianity is the dominant religion in the United States, it has a huge impact on society. That dominance is currently ending. This decade is when that dominance and influence begin to subside.

So, where are we going religiously? First of all, there will still be religions as people search for answers. People will continue to look outside of themselves for spiritual sustenance. However, the answers are all within, but it's not an easy journey to look within. It's so much easier to let someone else tell you the truth. So, people will continue to go to religious services for a few more generations. And just as today, not everyone will go.

The good news is that people will become more spiritual as the old souls spread the truth. I've already told you some of that truth, but I'll give you a few more nuggets. This is no one's first rodeo – first lifetime. We are all on a long journey to evolve our souls. How we choose to evolve our souls is our free choice. This means there is no judgment, and everything is perfect. That said, karma is real, and choices have ramifications.

The end result of our journey always (or nearly always) leads to the same outcome: enlightenment. And what is enlightenment? A complete recognition that you are one with God. And how is it possible for our journey to always lead to enlightenment? Because God is inside us, and the core of God is love, which is our core as well. So, we are all being guided toward love, even if it doesn't always appear that way. Eventually, that is where the journey leads.

Once we begin to wake up as a society regarding spiritual truth, education will become much more humane. This is another cultural shift. Instead of an indoctrination from grades one through twelve, children will be given much more freedom to learn what they want. There will be a plethora of experimentation regarding education. Some schools will not even have teachers, where students learn together and mentor each other.

Students will get the opportunity to spend more time learning about what excites their passion and less of what does not interest them. It will be a more natural way to learn, and by the time someone is eighteen, or perhaps twenty-five, they will have had an ample education and be ready for a profession.

Sports will also evolve. There will be more sports, which is a trend that has already begun. People will use their creativity to invent new sports. There will be more new sports that allow co-ed competition. This will have the added benefit of bringing the sexes closer together and will be highly popular.

Professional sports will begin to wane as people spend more of their time living their lives rather than watching others live theirs. Plus, professional sports tend to be money-based and star-based,

Chapter Four: Cultural Shift

which will begin to lose its appeal. As a society, we will want to move away from mega-stars and billionaires, toward something that is more inclusive for everyone. Many will find more satisfaction in participating than watching.

Professional sports will also lose customers as people have less money to attend professional events. Also, colleges will begin a period of decline (many colleges will close), which will reduce the allure of watching collegiate athletics.

The next decade will be one of hardship for many, which will reduce the amount of leisure time for watching sports. This will be a trend that is hard to turn around. I don't know if the Superbowl will end, but the number of viewers will be far less at the end of this decade. Will professional sports survive in its current form? I'm not sure, but it is unlikely.

One of the reasons sports will lose its allure will be the advent of AI and virtual reality. Why watch a sporting event when you can experience virtual reality, which will be much more immersive and more fun? For instance, you will be able to attend a virtual reality event that seems real, or you can watch a passive sporting event on a screen. Which would you choose? Trust me, there will be no comparison, and professional sports will slowly die from a lack of demand.

AI and virtual reality will also usher in a plethora of creativity. Millions of people will be self-employed, creating content using AI and virtual reality. If you think TikTok is popular today, just wait.

As the economy hits a wall and begins to flounder, materialism will lose its allure. Shopping till you drop will be replaced by a new trend of simplicity. Ironically, this will make people more social. If you are no longer concerned with acquiring stuff, then you will have more time to do other things, such as socializing.

More human interaction will lead to less judgment and the elimination of racism. This will be enhanced by the consciousness shift. The new communities that form will be the first to adopt these cultural changes and will set an example that proliferates throughout the world. America will continue to be a place that leads the way and is looked to for innovation in both products and ideas.

More human interaction within communities will also lead to sexual taboos being uprooted. Sexuality will be seen as something more than just used for reproduction, or between married people. There will be less condemnation and moral judgment toward those who do not conform to so-called societal sexual standards. Sexuality will be viewed from a new context of individual preference.

Perhaps the biggest coming change to culture over the next few decades will be the shift away from the idea of individual accomplishment and achievement. Today, humanity is fixated on the idea that the most important people are those who have the most accomplishments. In fact, today, we judge everyone based on their behavior and acheivements.

Celebrities, athletes, mega-stars, politicians, doctors, lawyers, and corporate moguls are all lauded as being successful. Soon, this will begin to diminish, and we will begin to recognize that successful people are not more special than anyone else. Instead, everyone will be recognized as special. Being human will take on a new connotation. Everyone who is here will be considered special. We will recognize that we are lucky to be here, and that everyone has a role to play.

Chapter Five

HEALTHCARE SHIFT

Most healthcare in the future will be energy-based (Note that when I use the term energy in this chapter, I am also referring to frequency). Instead of using biological medicine (pharmaceuticals) and surgery for healing, energy healing will steadily displace these modalities. This shift is already underway, but it will take generations to transition over to energy healing completely. Holistic healers have been using energy healing for decades, but it is about to go mainstream.

Could surgery be completely replaced by energy healing? Yes, because consciousness has no limitations. However, learning how to use our consciousness for all healing requirements will take a few generations.

Science is beginning to discover that the body is comprised of energy fields. Every organ has its own energy field and its own frequency, and the body itself has an energy field and frequency. The reason why these energy fields exist is because everything is vibrating energy, all the way down to the cellular level. Manipulating these vibrations (frequencies) has the ability to heal.

There are two facts that mainstream medicine is starting to recognize. The first is that nutrition (food, herbs, and essential oils) has much more healing power than is understood. The second is that energy healing can heal anything.

Nutrition and energy will be the two dominant healing modalities in the future. Gone will be the days of pharmaceutical drugs and surgery. Although, in our lifetime, we will only see the beginning of this shift.

It's ironic that some of the first doctors in antiquity said to let food be thy medicine. We have ignored that advice. In fact, as a civilization, we still haven't figured it out. However, it won't be long now before people use food, along with herbs and essential oils to cure diseases that today are considered incurable.

I thought that perhaps the COVID-19 epidemic would alert the public to the power of using nutrition as a preventative. There were a few voices informing people what to take to boost their immune systems, but alas, the MSM (mainstream media) largely ignored these voices. Many Americans wore a mask as a preventative based on the advice from the MSM, but did not take any supplements as a preventative to boost their immune systems. I took five supplements based on advice from Dr. Todd Ovokaitys, who is one of the rare doctors who have focused on preventative medicine.

Once the public recognizes the power of nutrition for healing and illness prevention, it will shift society's views on health and healthcare. Good health and nutrition will become all the rage, and eating a nutritionally poor diet will lose its appeal.

It's interesting that the COVID-19 virus will be the event that triggers society's shift into a new era of healthcare. This virus is impacting healthcare and, specifically, our personal health. There is a recognition that those who did not take the vaccine and relied on their immune system did fine. If there is another virus pandemic, many will rely on their immune system instead of a vaccine.

It's become clear that nutrition has the potential to support our immune system to prevent a virus from making us sick. However, few people in the medical community are speaking out about nutrition as an immune system booster. This approach has not yet made its way to the mainstream, but it soon will.

If our civilization were a bit more advanced, we would know what to ingest to enhance our immune system against a virus. In

Chapter Five: Healthcare Shift

fact, in the future, this is exactly what we will do. Armed with a strong immune system, we will not fear contracting any virus. Thus, a vaccine will not be needed. In fact, in the future, no vaccines will be needed. This probably won't happen in our lifetime, but future generations will likely not use vaccines and will be much healthier than our generation.

Nutrition (and supplementation) will be the first thing to make a powerful shift in society's beliefs around healthcare (eating to live instead of living to eat). Energy healing won't be far behind. There was a Star Trek movie where they placed an energy device on someone's forehead (you could see the blinking lights as it did its work). That is a good representation of how energy healing will occur in the future.

There will be many different types of energy healing in the future. Some will be from machines and devices, and some will be directly from a human healer to a human patient. In fact, it is possible to be healed by another human over vast distances. A healer can be on the other side of the world from the patient. This is also called remote healing.

There are many advantages to using energy healing instead of our current biological focus. For instance, energy healing is a lot less expensive than biological healing. Plus, the recovery time for energy healing is much shorter, often instantaneous. Also, energy healing is ideal for preventing disease because energy can be used to rebalance our energy fields before they cause illness.

The key to replacing biological healing with energy healing is tapping into our quantum abilities. This is a term that is somewhat new for humanity, but everyone will know about it soon. Quantum energy is the fundamental building block of life. Scientists are only now beginning to understand quantum energy. Today, they call it quantum physics, but their understanding is still at an elementary level. Thankfully, it is now possible for scientists on this planet to begin to understand quantum energy, also called quantum consciousness.

Soon, scientists will begin experimenting with consciousness. Ironically, what scientists have considered impossible – that consciousness is measurable – will be proven possible. It will open up a whole new field of science. It will be called the physics of consciousness. As I write these words, there is no such thing. Only old souls in the metaphysical movement know about it. But, watch with wonder as it appears on the scene and proves everything that I am writing in this chapter.

What scientists will need to do, as they begin to study the physics of consciousness, is to figure out that all matter is conscious, and that all matter is connected on a quantum level. They haven't figured this out yet, but they are getting close. They have figured out that particles can exist in two places simultaneously, but they don't understand how. What they don't understand yet is that the particles are conscious, and that consciousness has no limitations, such as remaining in one place at a time.

Scientists have also discovered quantum entanglement, whereby two particles in different locations are somehow connected. Again, science does not understand how this can occur. If you move one particle that is entangled with another, the other one automatically moves, no matter how far the distance. This is also due to the interconnectedness of consciousness.

On a quantum level, consciousness can transform cells. This transformation includes changing from an imperfect state to a perfect state. When this occurs, voila, you get instant healing. How does this occur? It's very similar to entanglement. The healer uses a quantum state to entangle their consciousness with that of the patient. The patient can be next to the healer or across the world. The healer then identifies the problem and rectifies it by manipulating the entangled consciousness.

Chapter Five: Healthcare Shift

I have a friend who is a healer who has done this many times. She is one of thousands on this planet who perform energy healing. She wanted me to make sure that I mentioned that she doesn't do the healing, nor does any energy healer. She might be called a healer, but she doesn't do the healing. She is only a conduit who connects the quantum energy so that it can flow into the patient. The energy does not reside in the healer. It is the energy of the Creator that flows through her and then into the patient.

An energy healer doesn't need to do anything more than direct the energy to the spot that needs healing. Then the energy is intelligent enough to do the healing. The energy is intelligent because it is conscious. It knows what needs to be done. In the future, most people will be able to heal themselves using their innate body to direct intelligent energy consciousness to what needs healing. This is already occurring today.

Energy healing is advanced medicine. What we call medicine today is quite primitive compared to what is possible. For instance, scientists today are physically manipulating DNA using CRISPR technology. With quantum energy healing, DNA can be manipulated with intelligent consciousness. This is the future of healthcare.

In the near future, parents will argue over whether to use an energy healer or mainstream medicine. People will soon have an option. In fact, they already do, although good energy healers are not easy to find.

Over time, as those studying the physics of consciousness make discoveries, mainstream medicine will invent devices that replace the need for energy healers. These devices will be able to manipulate cells in the body by changing their vibration (frequency). Cells are conscious, so as they are manipulated, the consciousness of the cells are changed. It is another form of healing, but essentially produces the same results as energy healing from a healer.

The Path Forward

While we wait for science to discover the building blocks of life (quantum consciousness), many humans will be a few steps ahead. People today can already manipulate their own DNA on a quantum level. Humans are becoming more quantum. This is all early innings, and few understand what I am writing about, but in the near future, it will be all the rage.

As humanity begins to shift spiritually, people will become more quantum. This shift into quantumness will have a profound impact on our health, both our ability to remain healthy and our ability to be healed.

What does it mean for a human to be more quantum? First of all, it gives us the ability to activate more of our DNA. This activation makes our DNA more dynamic. In a word, it makes our DNA more intelligent. Quantumness allows us to have more awareness and more acuity. It gives us access to our innate body, which, until now, has remained hidden from us. These are only a few characteristics of quantumness. There is much more to learn, such as the ability to translocate or slow down our aging process. Welcome to the rabbit hole.

On a quantum level with dynamic DNA, nothing is impossible from a healing perspective. Conversely, the body's immune system in a non-quantum state, without dynamic DNA, is severely limited. All it can do is react to attackers with a limited set of defenses. In a non-quantum state, the body is not intelligent enough to be dynamic. However, using quantum abilities, the body becomes dynamic and can do practically anything from a healing perspective.

A quantum human has DNA that is intelligent enough to perceive how it is being attacked, and then create a defense to prevent illness. This is not science fiction. There are already quantum humans on the planet today, and more and more people are activating their DNA to levels that allow quantum healing. It is a trend that is not going to stop.

Chapter Five: Healthcare Shift

Another amazing ability of quantum humans is the ability to slow the aging process. You can literally inform your DNA to limit how fast you age. The DNA can be told at what rate to age. While you likely won't get any younger (anything is possible in a quantum world!), you can slow aging significantly. Future generations will live much longer than we do using this intelligent DNA.

You may think this is crazy talk, but it is already occurring. Moreover, now that our DNA has changed, it is becoming more common for humans to display quantumness and this will steadily become even more common.

In the past, when someone had an instantaneous remission or their untreatable illness went away, that was quantum healing. Some rare people have always had these quantum abilities. Now it is going to begin to become more common.

Quantum abilities are not only used for healing and slowing aging. In fact, that will not likely be where you first experience it. Quantum reality has been hidden from us. For instance, we have 24 chromosomes and not 23. The 24th chromosome is quantum. We are in the process of turning that chromosome on. This is not yet known by the mainstream, and probably won't be for a while.

The 24th chromosome is extremely powerful. It changes everything. Currently, scientists think that our DNA is mostly composed of junk. They call this "junk DNA." They call it that because it doesn't appear to have any value. It looks like a big, jumbled mess. In reality, it is information that is unlocked by the 24th chromosome.

Guess what is in all of that jumbled mess? It's information about our past lives. And guess what happens when we unlock the 24th chromosome? We get access to that information, which is our Akashic records, and everything we have ever done as a soul. This will change most of us and make us better people.

The 24th chromosome is what will lead science to prove that God exists. Why? Because there is more information in our DNA than in all the books on the planet combined. And every cell in our body contains our DNA. If that isn't intelligent design, I don't know what is. This proof that God exists will occur around 2050, and the proof will be based on consciousness, quantum energy, and dynamic DNA.

Humans on this planet are only using about thirty percent of their DNA. Once we turn on our 24th chromosome, our DNA's efficiency will steadily rise to about thirty-five percent. That is quite a leap for mankind. At thirty-five percent, there will be very little illness. I don't know how many generations it will take for us to reach thirty-five percent as a civilization, but many humans will reach thirty-five percent in this lifetime. Quantum energy healers are already around thirty-five percent activated.

As more and more people become quantum humans, we are going to see dramatic changes in healthcare. Holistic healing centers will become common throughout the country. These will be staffed by energy healers who are quantum humans. What they will be accomplishing will eventually be replicated by machines and devices that can do the same thing – rebalance our energy fields and keep us healthy.

In the near future, it will not be uncommon for children to have the ability to diagnose illness by reading someone's energy field. Yes, these children will be quantum humans, and most of them will be energy healers.

Already today, we have energy healers throughout the country. Many of them have individual holistic practices that operate under the radar. They offer a vast array of healing modalities, including forms of nutrition. At some point, these individual practices will be displaced by larger holistic healing centers. That is when they will go mainstream.

Chapter Five: Healthcare Shift

The reason for these larger healing centers is that it is known that multiple people can heal more effectively when working together. They become a larger conduit. I know of a true story in which multiple people were healing someone remotely at a distant hospital, and they cured someone of cancer who was in the hospital bed next to the patient they were praying for. Somehow their prayers moved the energy into the entire room! The energy was intelligent enough to heal both patients. Such is the power of multiple healers working together.

Another major shift regarding health will be around diet and our food sources. Today, we eat a lot of processed foods and so-called junk food. That will steadily decline as we become more conscious. It will begin to make more sense for people to consume healthy food and avoid processed food.

As I mentioned earlier, natural food will start to be used to treat illness. From this trend, people will begin to grasp the importance of a healthy diet. I'm not saying that everyone will become a vegetarian or vegan, although those choices will become more common. But a shift away from processed foods will become the norm. It is my expectation that fast-food restaurants will become less popular and many will close. Over time, I expect all of them to disappear.

The diet that will become the norm will be to eat fresh food that has been recently harvested. We will want to consume food that is alive, such as fruits and vegetables in their raw form. In many communities, the majority of the food people consume will be grown locally. An improvement in diet and nutrition will have a profound impact on our overall healthn for the betterment of society.

If you want to get a head start on better health and cancer prevention, you can read my book, *Get Healthy, Stay Healthy*.

The Path Forward

Chapter Six

SPIRITUAL SHIFT

In the last chapter, I wrote about the new quantum human and how we are going to activate our DNA to higher levels. All of that content about the new quantum human could have been included in this chapter. The new quantum human can only occur through the expansion of consciousness, and that can't happen without impacting our spirituality.

To review, most humans only use about thirty percent of their DNA. At that level of activation, our quantumness is dormant. That is now changing. As a civilization, we are becoming more quantum and more multidimensional. As our DNA activation increases, our DNA becomes more quantum and multidimensional.

The truth is that we are multidimensional, quantum beings, and our quantumness is being hidden from us by our lack of spiritual awareness (which is correlated to our soul-body frequency). The good news is that humanity crossed a pivotal threshold in 2012, when humanity as a whole (the mass consciousness) reached a higher frequency. As a result, we can now access more of our multidimensional, quantum self. We now have the potential to become more of who we truly are – Gods-in-training.

That last sentence might be a new concept for some of you. Prepare yourself; there will be many more in this chapter. This is clearly a red pill type of chapter. You won't be coming away unscathed, but you will learn the truth.

Let's begin with this truth: the consciousness for our soul originates from the Creator. This origination embeds the Creator into our soul, and into us. In essence, there is no separation between our soul and the Creator. We are, in essence, one. Not only are we one with the Creator, but also with each other and all of life. There is no you, and there is no me. There is we. Individuated consciousness is an illusion. Interconnectedness is the truth. There is only oneness.

This oneness is the foundation of life. It is the foundation of our spirituality. It is the foundation of everything we do and will do. From this embedded oneness, the Creator then gives us the free will to evolve through free choice. However, there are limitations to our free will because of our connection to each other and our connection to the Creator. Ironically, this connection is actually an illusion because all there really is, is the Creator. Everything that appears separate from the Creator is an illusion. Yes, my friend, your separateness is an illusion. Smiley face. Exclamation point. Nothing exists outside of oneness.

What limits our free will is actually our ego getting in the way. If we were enlightened beings (and one day we will be), then we would live with a higher consciousness and be considered ascended masters. This level of consciousness is something we all aspire toward, even though this ambition of higher consciousness is not usually apparent.

The Creator oversees our development as a soul. Yes, we have free will to a certain extent, but like a strong parent, the Creator can't help being involved. The Creator assigns to each and every one of us an entourage of discarnate beings to watch over us. I used to think that everyone had at least one guardian angel, but I now think that everyone has several discarnate beings who watch over us.

What I do know is that everyone is dearly loved by the Creator and by those discarnate beings (you can call them angels if you want) who watch over us. And when I say dearly, consider it at a deep emotional level beyond our comprehension. When we

Chapter Six: Spiritual Shift

incarnate as human beings, we only have a cursory understanding of the level of love that exists for each human being from the other side of the veil – the etheric nonphysical reality.

We are truly loved on a deep, unconditional level. It is ironic that the love we seek in this lifetime already exists on another level. In other words, we seek something that we already have and think we don't. This is why, when people have near-death experiences, they usually want to stay on the other side and continue experiencing that deep feeling of love. That is who we truly are because that is our core – love.

This love originates with the Creator, who embeds it into all of the lifeforms that It creates. A good example of how this love flourishes is in the animal kingdom. Isn't it interesting that dog spelled backward is god? The unconditional love that a dog has for its owner is a reminder of the Creator's love for us.

So, when the Creator creates a new soul from Itself, it embeds into the soul Its core, which is love. That core of love will inevitably lead the soul to evolve and become God-like. This is why we are Gods-in-training.

Until 2012, it wasn't that important for most of you to read this. Until then, only a small percentage of the planet was passionate about soul growth. And those souls, such as myself, found a way to find out this truth about the soul. For the rest of you, it remained a secret. But now, everything has changed, and now, you too, can evolve your soul to levels that previously were not possible in this lifetime. You may doubt this, but by the end of this chapter, you will have a better understanding of what I am explaining.

As the soul vibrates higher and activates the DNA to higher levels, the possibilities for soul evolvement are quite amazing. For instance, if you activate the DNA one level higher, that goes with you into your next lifetime. If you activate it two levels higher, you take that, too, and on and on.

It's hard to explain the opportunity that exists at this current time. We can evolve our souls at a rapid pace that previously would require many lifetimes. Many of us will become ascended masters in this lifetime, a goal that has taken hundreds or thousands of lifetimes. Many of us will overcome karma that has existed for many, many lifetimes.

To be alive at this time is a blessing, and trust me when I say that is an understatement. Not only do we get to be the forefathers of the new era of humanity, but we get to evolve at a rapid rate that is quite rare.

In an earlier chapter, I said that the reason humanity was going to get better is because we were going to fall in love with each other. Now, you may doubt this, but many will watch it unfold. Where will this love come from? Our core. As the soul vibrates higher and we become more multidimensional, we will get closer to our inner connection to spirit, which is our higher self. We will feel compelled to seek a higher consciousness instead of our current preoccupation with our egoic lower consciousness: selfishness, anger, greed, lust, narcissism, hedonism, etc.

Humanity will feel a revulsion for our lower egoic consciousness and will strive toward creating a better world using higher consciousness. Again, this will be DNA-activated. It's not going to happen because humanity suddenly decides to create a better world. No, the Creator is making it happen on a cellular level, one person at a time.

The secrets are coming out! I've told you some in this chapter. Not only were we created from the Creator, but the Creator is embedded into our soul. We are dearly loved. We are eternal. Each

Chapter Six: Spiritual Shift

of us is evolving into a wiser, loving soul. The evolvement of the soul is inevitable because the Creator is involved in its outcome.

That last paragraph is not widely known at this time, but it will be. It is the truth, and the truth is coming out. It has to because as a civilization, we have passed the knowledge barrier (in 2019) – another truth that is not widely known. Science is now on the precipice of understanding consciousness and that everything is connected consciously. Once that is understood, the secrets can no longer be hidden.

Reincarnation is already understood in the East. It won't take much to spread that truth to the West after the physics of consciousness is understood. People will begin to change their beliefs. The Creator will be known, and religions will slowly die in their current form.

* * * * *

So, what is the coming spiritual shift? It is a shift away from accepting the beliefs of others and instead finding your own. No two people can have the same beliefs. Sure, two people can believe what I have written in this chapter, but not the specifics. There will always be differences. For this reason, the new spirituality will be for you to determine your own beliefs.

The big shift will be away from religions and away from group beliefs. Each individual will be allowed to determine their own beliefs, and their own spirituality. No longer will society indoctrinate children on what to believe. No longer will religion be passed on to the next generation.

Of course, this movement away from religions won't occur all at once; it will take another generation before most religions are either gone or become a shell of their former selves.

There is so much momentum now that nothing can stop humanity from turning on our 24th chromosome – our quantum chromosome. Many have already turned it on. Many are activating their DNA to higher levels. This is changing them. Instead of being ruled by lower consciousness, people are following a higher consciousness. They are reaching toward the truth, the love, and the light. They are reaching toward their highest ideals, but it's more than that. They are reaching toward their inner calling, which is a spiritual calling. They feel the truth, and they are drawn to it.

I've been writing new-age, metaphysical, spiritual books since 1991, but this is the first one where I can truly see humanity's destiny. We are going to awaken to our true selves. Not all at once, of course, but one at a time. And, as more and more people awaken, it will have a profound impact on humanity.

Now, what does it mean to awaken to our true selves? The starting point is a deep connection to our inner higher self. This is exemplified by remaining in a higher consciousness (unconditional love, compassion, empathy, integrity, truth, calmness, etc.) and avoiding a lower consciousness (anger, hatred, judgment, violence, lies, selfishness, hedonism, avariciousness, etc.). It is also exemplified by all of the qualities of being virtuous. This is not the common way we currently live as humans on this planet, but it is now our destiny. We will become more principled and prone to doing the right thing.

This may seem impossible, but if what I have written is true – that we are becoming quantum beings – then it isn't such a stretch. We will become highly intuitive and acutely sensitive to right and wrong. Again, this won't happen to everyone at once, but will steadily reverberate and increase throughout humanity.

Chapter Six: Spiritual Shift

Today, people stay in lower consciousness because they drown out the voice of intuition and their connection to their higher self. What happens to people is that they stop listening to their hearts. It becomes too hard, and they give up. It is much easier to give in to temptation and follow that little voice that says this will make you feel good. And after we give in too many times, our higher self and spirit guides recede. We lose touch with our guidance within and become dominated by our ego.

The good news is that our guidance system is being reborn. It's still there. It just needs to be listened to. A starting point is recognizing that life is more about being than doing. In other words, life is not about me; it's about we. We are here to help each other and not step on each other. The golden rule is, indeed, the path to follow: Do unto others as you would like to be treated. Thus, be empathetic and humble.

Notice that those are two virtuous words. Those are words of higher consciousness. That is the starting point for understanding that being is more important than doing. Today, we think that doing is everything. We "do" in order to accomplish, so that we will be respected, but it's a trap, and pulls us away from the truth. We honor and praise people for their actions because we want to be honored and praised. We admire people for their actions so that our actions are admired. Occasionally, we will give accolades for character, but it is usually always entwined with their actions.

If you are wise, you will see that humanity is at a significant transition point in history, where we change from recognizing actions to recognizing character (integrity and virtue). While this transition is only beginning, it will take some time to separate actions from character.

In the distant future, character will be monumentally more important than actions. Why? Because the core of our soul is character, and that is what we are all striving to improve.

When this lifetime is over, we will look back on how we lived our life using a life review. We will not look at the actions that helped us to be successful in the eyes of society. Instead, we look back on how we treated others, and how we treated ourselves. We will review our character.

Can you see how momentous this transition point is for humanity? We are now going to begin giving character more importance, a lot more importance. And this is the very thing the soul desires to improve. So, we are creating a much better world.

As you can imagine, life will take on a much more spiritual tone. If character becomes more important than achievements and actions, then how we treat each other will change. People will now be revered simply for being a human being. We will acknowledge that *everyone* is a God-in-training. Again, this won't happen all at once and will take a few generations. But it begins now.

Perhaps the most important change to humanity, which is also a spiritual shift, is that love will begin to permeate throughout the world. Remember when I said that we would begin to fall in love with each other? Well, it's coming soon and will only get stronger over time. Love is going to liberate humanity.

Love is going to be all-encompassing and abundant. You won't be able to get away from it. The Creator is unleashing it on this planet. That's what happens when the truth is released. Once you *know* that you are a piece of God, the Creator, and eternal, it changes the way you approach life. This new approach will open the connection to your higher self. That connection is like a giant light bulb, releasing the light of God, which is love.

So, as everyone's light bulb begins to shine, the light of God – which is love – is released. It may begin slowly, but it won't be long before it is released to the world in a big way. When? I think it will be noticeable by the end of the decade.

Chapter Six: Spiritual Shift

Currently, most of us have DNA that is limited and can only exhibit fixed characteristics. This is now changing as our DNA becomes activated and more dynamic. This dynamic, multidimensional DNA is incredibly powerful. As stated previously, humans will become more quantum, which is to say, multidimensional – existing in two places simultaneously. If a particle can do it, then surely our soul can do it, too!

In a quantum state, DNA can do nearly anything. So, expect to see what are currently perceived to be miracles. These miracles will intrigue scientists enough to study what is happening and will lead them to the physics of consciousness. However, it will also lead many on a spiritual quest to understand the soul and consciousness.

Consciousness has always intrigued human curiosity. Once consciousness begins to exhibit new qualities, it will lead people to question their beliefs about consciousness. For instance, can consciousness self-heal or slow the aging process? Indeed, it can, and if it can do that, what else can it do?

Big questions will be asked. Is consciousness the soul? Is the soul contained within the body? What does the soul take with it when it leaves the body? Is the soul connected to something more? Can we really be part of a consciousness that is bigger than us? Where does our consciousness come from? How does intuition work? Can the soul be in two places at the same time? Can DNA dynamically heal itself?

Humanity has never asked these questions on a large scale, but that is about to change. Religious beliefs will be questioned and reevaluated. People will demand answers and demand a thorough vetting of what society believes. No more will people accept the beliefs that have been handed down for centuries.

The Path Forward

When a small child heals everyone in their classroom to such an extent that no one gets sick for the entire year, it will not be ignored or considered a miracle. It will be acknowledged that a child in that class balanced the energy fields of all the students using his or her consciousness as a conduit. Society will begin to recognize the truth of what is happening with our consciousness – that it is changing.

It will be one small step at a time, but it won't be long before our beliefs are radically transformed regarding what consciousness can do. Once this begins, our spiritual beliefs will be upended. No longer will people believe that we are separate from each other, or that God favors one religion over another. All of humanity will be perceived as equals because consciousness has no bias.

What I am writing about has huge ramifications for society. If you are reading it before the changes begin, then perhaps you are treating it as a fantasy. If you are reading it during or after, it will have a more potent emotional punch. The changes that are occurring and will occur are profound. We are living through a time of revolutionary spiritual change. The switch has been flipped, and now change is the watchword for our future.

All aspects of our lives from now on will be in a process of dynamic change. The reason for this is because of the changes to our consciousness and DNA. Steadily, as society gains more and more understanding of our consciousness, our lives will be impacted from these truths. Spiritual truths will steadily unfold, and then these truths will transform society.

Initially, the changes to society will come as people become more aware that society is unjust, with the government and corporations having too much power. That will begin a cascade of shifting beliefs toward a more humane society. But that will just be the tip of the iceberg. Then we will begin to see how people are changing by

Chapter Six: Spiritual Shift

activating more of their DNA. Then we will begin to accept that consciousness is much different than we thought we knew.

These initial changes will force people to rethink many of their beliefs. Those who try to hold on to their old beliefs will find themselves as part of a shrinking minority of disbelievers. Society will surge ahead with new beliefs and new ways of living. However, once we think we know everything new that is occurring, more new consciousness attributes will appear and shift society once again. Change will become so rampant that settling into a new way of life will become difficult, if not impossible, for many years to come

* * * * *

As I said earlier, as the truth is released, people will question their beliefs. This will upend spirituality as we know it today. People will be forced to find a new method of spirituality. If they try to run to a religion, they will find that it is insufficient and is in denial of what is happening. Religions will try to create a spiritual foundation for people, but all they will end up doing is denying the truth. Eventually, people will be drawn to the truth, and religions will wither away.

As people become more psychic and acutely intuitive, a major spiritual shift will unfold, with belief systems being questioned and reevaluated. There will be a renaissance of spiritual understanding. The concepts that I am writing about in this book will be studied. People will go back and listen to what Jane Roberts channeled in the 1960s (Seth) and other modern esoteric teachings, such as Kryon channeled by Lee Carroll, Bashar channeled by Darryl Anka, and the Guides channeled by Paul Selig.

This spiritual renaissance will not occur all at once. For our generation, many will be able to do telepathy, self-healing, illness prevention, and slow down our aging process. But few will be able to translocate their body from one location to another, or create material objects out of thin air. These advanced quantum abilities will eventually be possible to many as we get more DNA activation in future generations.

With more DNA activation, humans get more access to their multidimensional abilities. This is already occurring today, and especially with those born since 2012. As each year passes, DNA activation increases. The old souls are already feeling this outcome. The biggest change is a stronger frequency of love and compassion toward others. This new frequency will steadily lead us toward world peace with less violence and war.

As more of our DNA activates, it will be easier for us to connect with our higher self and our innate body. This will enhance the spiritual shift that is currently underway. Steadily, society will become more and more aware about the truth of their soul. The percentage of people who *know* that they are a soul in a human body will steadily increase.

The bad news is that this will not happen for everyone, and many will remain stuck in their old beliefs regarding duality (good versus evil). Those stuck in their old beliefs will cause our social problems to linger for a few more generations. But it will become apparent within another decade that we are making progress and that what I have written is accurate.

It will not be easy for society to change, although it is now inevitable. Mankind (or rather, humankind) will come to embrace love as the centerpiece of humanity (along with individual free will and individual freedom). Society will recognize that every human is a part of the Creator and that their core is love. This will take some time, but it's coming. Love will begin to rise within

Chapter Six: Spiritual Shift

humanity. It will take some time to become apparent, but that will be the new creed.

Once love permeates throughout humanity, racism, war, and injustice will be mere fragments of what they are today. This is not a fairytale. This is the Creator's plan for humanity. This is the destined outcome, and the eventual outcome.

Your part – now that you have been exposed to this knowledge – is to find a way to release more love onto this planet and thereby speed up the transition toward enlightenment. However, since this outcome is inevitable, you can just "be" and thereby allow the process to unfold. The Creator will not judge you or your decisions, whichever way you decide to help. Judgment can only be done to yourself. You are your own judge. If you think it is your duty to help mankind, then do it. If not, then that is okay, too.

Most humans, as they become aware of the grand plan for this planet, will feel compelled to help – I know I do. Once you find out that your core is love and that your soul is a part of the Creator, there is usually an "ah-ha" moment where you recognize that the only meaning in life is to help the Creator in any way that you can – to find a way to be in service. Or, at the very least, become reverent of the Creator and not get in the way.

Life can be very difficult, and helping the Creator may not always be your first priority, especially if you are struggling with your personal life. The Creator understands this and allows us our free choice. So, do what you can to help humanity, but don't make it a personal burden. Remember, the Creator allows complete free choice without judgment. Whatever you choose to do is okay.

The Creator loves us unconditionally and allows us to choose our own unique journey to enlightenment. As humanity evolves, we will learn to have this same attitude toward others.

It may not appear that life is perfect, and that everything that happens in life is perfect. However, that is the truth because the Creator can only know perfection. So, I trust the perfection in God's plan, but I also try to make myself a better person and to become more spiritually aware. I hope that you, too, have the goal of becoming a better person. I think that is the best way of helping humanity.

Life is a bit of a Catch-22. Life is perfect, but we are trying to become better people and more spiritually aware. If you don't try, then life will appear to be imperfect and quite frustrating. The more you try, the more rewarding it will be.

Finally, never forget the blessing that this lifetime truly is. Be grateful, be humble, and love others as much as you can. And always remember that service is the highest ideal one can hold. Ultimately, we are in service to one another. Again, it's not about me, it's about we.

* * * * *

I want to end this chapter by explaining why people avoid the truth, and why most people will initially deny the truth when it is released this decade. This planet is a school, and its foundation is duality (good and evil) in tandem with free will. That foundation is now changing (the mass consciousness has decided to awaken), but the lingering effects of duality will not easily go away.

When we come here (via incarnation), we assume a personality structure in order to learn lessons (note that these personalities are chosen by us in advance of this lifetime). This personality structure requires that we forget who we are (eternal souls) in order for us to assume these personalities. They are fake, but they appear to

Chapter Six: Spiritual Shift

be real. The illusion is so convincing that people believe that these personalities are real. Bob believes he is Bob. Karen believes she is Karen. You probably believe that your personality is who you are. It's not. Your soul is real, but it is much different from your current personality structure.

Awakening to the truth requires that you recognize that this world is an illusion and that the true you is someone completely different. That shock is not something that everyone can handle. Moreover, that recognition is not easily achieved and is much easier to deny. The personality would much rather focus on its personal happiness and the life it has created or is trying to create. The personality would much rather remain with its current beliefs than veer off into woo-woo land and recognize the truth.

Once a glimpse of the truth is seen (and for most of you, that has already happened), the personality would much rather remain with its current beliefs and current life. It is frightening to question your beliefs and the impact that such a change could have. All of your relationships and your job could be impacted. So, staying with your current beliefs is a much safer choice. Thus, denial of the truth is the expected reaction and will remain common for many years to come.

The denial of the truth will remain the norm this decade. However, once the truth is released, there will be a steady increase in its acceptance. Moreover, even those in denial will be quite aware of this truth and that more and more people are accepting it. It will become a trend that is unstoppable.

Soon, it will no longer be easy to ignore the truth and pretend that this world is all there is to reality, or that your religion is a sufficient form of spirituality. Until this decade, questioning the status quo of your spiritual foundation was never a question. That won't be the case for much longer. You will be forced to choose:

The Path Forward

1) Stick with your beliefs, or 2) Begin to question them and all of the ramifications that come with that decision.

We have reached the end. Sorry for the harsh red pill, but the truth is coming out, and it is time for that outcome.

Afterword

There are two additional sources I highly recommend that are related to this material. The first is my AI video titled *How to Solve All the World's Problems*. It will soon be on my website, www.dondurrett.com. That video is an explanation of unity consciousness.

The second source is my book titled *Post America: A New Constitution*. It is available on Amazon in paperback, digital, and audio formats. This new constitution offers ideas for reorganizing society. Many of these ideas will come in handy after society breaks down and needs to be reorganized.

Book Review Request

If you enjoyed this book and think that others would benefit, please write a review on Amazon. Most readers rely on reviews to make their decision.

The Path Forward

www.ingramcontent.com/pod-product-compliance
Lightning Source LLC
Chambersburg PA
CBHW071409290426
44108CB00014B/1749